THE ULTIMATE
GUIDE
TO BEING A
CHRISTIAN
IN COLLEGE

Also by Jeff Baxter

*Together: Adults and Teenagers
Transforming the Church*

THE ULTIMATE GUIDE TO BEING A CHRISTIAN IN COLLEGE

JEFF BAXTER

ZONDERVAN

ZONDERVAN.com/
AUTHORTRACKER
follow your favorite authors

ZONDERVAN

The Ultimate Guide to Being a Christian in College
Copyright © 2009, 2012 by Jeff Baxter

Previously published (in an unrevised form) as
Following Jesus into College and Beyond

This title is also available as a Zondervan ebook.
Visit www.zondervan.com/ebooks.

Requests for information should be addressed to:

Zondervan, *Grand Rapids, Michigan* 49530

Library of Congress Cataloging-in-Publication Data

CIP applied for: ISBN 978-0-310-73223-5

Cover design: Micah Kandros Design
Interior design & composition: Greg Johnson/Textbook Perfect

Printed in the United States of America

12 13 14 15 16 17 /DCI/ 20 19 18 17 16 15 14 13 12 11 10 9 8 7 6 5 4 3 2 1

To the Next Generation:

May your faith in Jesus move from just surviving
to thriving during these important years.

CONTENTS

FOREWORD

by Chap Clark

This is a good book. But more than that, it's a really important book. If you're preparing for college or just beginning your college years, I hope you'll not only read this book, but go through it slowly and carefully, taking notes and talking about it with those who know and love you.

Do you have any idea how many high school disciples—I mean the ones most people consider to be "real Christians": those who take Jesus seriously, who sincerely intend to follow him for the rest of their lives, and who have made sacrificial choices in the face of strong opposition because of their faith—end up feeling, in the months or years after high school, that they've either let their faith slip into the background of their lives, or simply blown it off altogether? There's disagreement over exact figures, but everybody agrees the number is huge. The question is this: As you make the transition into college and beyond, how will you not only keep your faith, but also flourish as a powerful, committed, vibrant follower of Jesus? That's what this book is all about.

Jeff Baxter wrote this book to help you grab hold of all that God has for you. *The Ultimate Guide to Being a Christian in College* is an honest, clear, and practical guide that will give you the chance to really soar as you explore Christ's unique calling for you. If you sincerely go after what's here, you will be changed for three reasons:

1. Jeff gets it. He has spent many years moving in and around the lives of high school and college students. He has spent lots of time (and money) to get a top-level education that helps him understand how growing up today is different than it was even ten years ago. And Jeff has dedicated himself to pursuing Christ with everything he's got. Even though he's far from perfect (I know him pretty well), he knows the Christian life that usually gets talked about can be far different from how it works out in real life. Jeff gets it and he cares. You are safe and respected in his hands.

2. Most of what's in this book will probably be new to you—and to your parents, friends, and even your youth leader—but you need to know it. As you read this book, be sure to take notes, pray, and open yourself up to others who can walk with you through the issues Jeff highlights. The new insights he shares will give you a deeper awareness of who you are, what trips you up and why, and where you're going as the person God created and called. This is *not* a "textbook"; it is a friend and a guide that can help you see more clearly where you are headed and where your steps are landing along the way.

3. If you will read carefully and listen carefully to God through the Scriptures, by his Spirit, and in the words of others, **you will discover that the gospel is more about the place God is taking you than the places you have been.** The more you can cultivate a forward-leaning trust in Jesus, especially compared with a faith that worries or compromises or is shackled by the past, the more you will see and experience the power of God working in your life.

You see, our lives and our growth are not for us; they are for our Lord. Life comes down to a single adventure—following God's lead as he brings in his kingdom and living out this quest alongside all who have heard and responded to his call. As you grow into the man or woman God created and bought to new life through his Spirit, this book will be an important friend along the way.

Chap Clark, PhD
Professor of Youth, Family, and Culture
Fuller Theological Seminary

ACKNOWLEDGMENTS

(for the people who made this thing happen)

I am grateful to so many people for helping with this revised and updated book. First and foremost, thank you Jesus Christ for being my everything. May your Name be glorified!

Laurie, my wife, for your love and support. You make me a better man because of your love for the Lord.

Lillian, Levi, and Lara—my beautiful kids—for allowing me to share the principles of this book and for showing me grace when I blow it.

Thank you Jacque Alberta and the whole Zondervan team for helping refresh my thoughts on the next generation and putting them into print with updates and additions.

Thank you Foothills Bible Church for allowing me to use my gifts in ministry. I appreciate your partnership to reach and disciple all generations with the gospel.

Finally, a big thanks to YOU, the reader, for taking the time to think about the words on these pages and applying the principles to your life. May God be with you during this important time in your spiritual journey.

For more resources and articles from Dr. Jeff Baxter, go to his blog
SacredOutfitter.blogspot.com

INTRODUCTION

(or The Part Most of Us Don't Read but Really Should)

I'm excited to get out into the real world and become who God intends me to be, but I'm extremely nervous. What if I fail? How will I know if I'm doing what I should? I pray about my future a lot, that God will help me to make the right decisions.

— Jaclyn, 17

Hi, I'm Jeff—the guy who wrote this book. I'm thrilled you're reading it because I believe it has the potential to alter your life for good and grow you closer to God as you move into a real-world adventure.

The Ultimate Guide to Being a Christian in College is written for high school students and recent graduates who are making the transition from life in high school to life in the real world. Whether your next step is college, a job, or something else, my goal is to help you ask the right questions and really think about what it means to follow Jesus. It's my hope that this book will also be helpful to parents, youth pastors, teachers, and others who seek to partner with students as they make the all-important transition from high school to life after graduation.

I probably don't need to tell you that the life of the average high school student has changed dramatically over the past decade or two. Adults love to say, "When I was in high school, I used to ..." Doesn't it drive you crazy when you hear that? Well, times have changed too much for this one-liner to have much value. With all

of the challenges and potential temptations connected with Facebook,
Internet porn, advertisements, date
rape, terrorism, depression, cutting,
not to mention various pressures and
stresses—it's a brand-new world out
there. Did I mention it's stressful? I'm
not all that old, but I'm very aware

> *You're about to begin a new chapter in your life — a clean, new page. Allow God to pen the words of this chapter into a beautiful masterpiece of worship.*
>
> *—Ryan, 24*

that the pressures you face are vastly different than the ones I faced
when I was in high school. It's much more difficult to negotiate those
treacherous waters than it used to be.

This book is all about helping you stay afloat in those waters. It's
filled with quotes from teenagers just like you who are preparing to
head out into the world, as well as advice from college students and
other twentysomethings who've been through what you're facing
now. These quotes were taken from surveys I sent out to hundreds
of high school and college students. I also draw from my years in
ministry—both inside and outside the local church—and do my
best to provide you with insights I've gathered as an adult who's
not only a student of Jesus and culture, but has also worked with
teenagers, college students, and twentysomethings for many years.

I hope you'll think of this book as a buffet (or a reference handbook). I've tried to set a table with a wide variety of foods that can
nourish your soul. So with help from our heavenly Father, come to
the book-buffet. Take whatever you like—maybe eat dessert first!
Leave what's not helpful, but eat till your heart's content. My prayer
is that the truths in this book will help you make a smooth transition into college and beyond.

Welcome to the Customize-Everything World

Have you noticed you can customize just about everything these
days? Think about it: Cars have custom designs from the front
bumper to the muffler. (And that's just the exterior!) If you have a

cell phone (and if you don't, you'll need one before you leave for college), you know you can choose your own cover, ring tone, and display, morphing it into personalized eye candy. Your computer's desktop is arranged just the way you like it. You can customize your Facebook page until it stands out from those of your friends.

> *I'm really excited for everything—college, family, and ministry—and yet sometimes I get caught up in thinking I can't be used now while I'm still in high school. But I can. I don't have to wait for college to start looking for opportunities to serve others.*
>
> —Haylee, 15

And how about coffee? I love coffee. I remember when the only choice you had to make when ordering was regular or decaf, but that's not how it goes today. Now it's nothing to say, "I'll take a grande, low-fat, iced caramel macchiato with extra caramel drizzle." (Okay, maybe forget the low-fat part.) I was so proud the last time I ordered a latte because all the boxes on the side of the cup were checked. They even wrote my name on the side. It was customized, baby!

But what about your life? Can that be customized as well? As you make the transition from high school to what's next—which might mean college, work, or both—you have a great opportunity to customize your life, to make it your own. This might be incredibly exciting as you've been waiting, even longing, for years to enter the "real world." Or you may find it mostly terrifying—all the responsibilities that come with the adult world might have you hiding in your closest while reading this book.

Most likely it's a combination of feelings, and your excitement level changes depending on the day. But before you decide to make like a baby bird and fly the coop, you'll want to be sure your feathers are developed and you have the skills to take that jump. Otherwise, gravity will take over, and down you'll go—which only brings stressful times and deep wounds.

> *I'm kind of nervous that I am pretty much on my own now. I have to grow up and take life on as an adult.*
>
> —Stephanie, 18

I hope this book will help you grow your feathers long and strong so you can steadily soar at ten thousand feet (and avoid most of the bumps and bruises along the way)!

The Interruption

Have you ever been interrupted right in the middle of something? Maybe you were doing some homework and your little sister came walking into your room. Or maybe you're a songwriter, and you were on a roll when your best friend called.

Interruptions are distracting. They slow things down. Once, my oldest sister interrupted my freshman basketball team's practice. It was right around my birthday (December 10), and she was home from college. For some reason she decided to show up dressed as Mrs. Claus, and she brought birthday cupcakes. When she walked in the gym, everyone stopped what they were doing. The varsity, junior varsity, and freshman players—they all stood still, held their basketballs, and waited to see who Mrs. Claus intended to visit. She waltzed over and gave the cupcakes to me. I love my sister. But at the time, her impromptu celebration was an interruption of my free-throw practice—and a new addition to my list of top-ten most-embarrassing moments.

Your transition into adulthood might seem like one great big interruption. It's distracting, upsetting, out-of-place, exciting, and nerve-racking all at the same time. As one twentysomething explained, "Young adults are in the middle: not married, not old enough, not in high school. We're in this 'ugh' stage." I'll bet sometimes you want to be a full-fledged adult so bad you could scream. You're tired of people treating you like a child. But this phase of life you're going through is distinct, unique, and normal. Lots of changes are happening, and many people have mixed feelings about these changes.

Take a look at what some high school students had to say about the transition to college and beyond. (You'll find quotes from other students scattered throughout this book.) See if you can identify with any of them:

> *I'm more than ready to leave the high school scene, to enter the real world and meet people who are a little more focused and a little more spiritually and emotionally mature. I'm not at all nervous because I know God will take care of me, but I'm really ready to move on to better things.*
>
> —Shae, 18

> *I'm very nervous because I have no clue what I will do after high school. I know I shouldn't be nervous because God holds my life in his hands and has a plan for me.*
>
> —Brooke, 17

> *I have mixed emotions about becoming an adult. I'm excited to see what God brings into my life but very nervous because I don't really know what's going to happen. It's a great adventure.*
>
> —Annabel, 15

As you look toward the future, maybe you feel pure excitement, or maybe you feel pure terror. Perhaps you connect with the mixture of nervousness and excitement Annabel describes. No matter what you're feeling, I hope this book will help calm your nerves and energize your spirit as you head into this great adventure of following Jesus.

When Does Your Real World Begin?

In the United States you're legally considered an adult on the day you turn eighteen. Once you're eighteen, a variety of privileges and responsibilities are yours: You can vote, own property, buy tobacco, marry without parental consent, be tried as an adult if you commit a crime, and even buy things from infomercials on late-night TV. But is this really what adulthood is all about?

My hunch? You already know there's more to being an adult than simply reaching a particular birthday. There are more questions to answer, more things to figure out—especially if you want to become a mature adult who follows Jesus.

I'm writing this book with the prayer that it will help you figure out how to become an adult who is mature in your Christian faith. You don't

> *I have no idea what I want to do with my life, so I'm nervous about making the wrong decisions and messing up my future.*
>
> — Justine, 17

become one automatically when you turn eighteen; you become one when you've fully engaged the journey toward maturity. Sooner or later everyone will become an adult—I want to help you get there before you're forty years old. Trust me; I know some forty-year-olds who haven't made it yet. (I'm sure you know some too.)

In this book we'll explore three critical themes of what it means for you to enter the world after high school and grow into a mature, Jesus-following adult.

In each of these areas (or legs), we'll tackle important questions that focus on what awaits you in life and in your faith. These fall under three main categories:

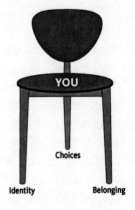

Leg One—Identity: Who am I? Who am I supposed to be, and what do I know to be true? Can I doubt sometimes?

Leg Two—Choices: Do my decisions matter? How much control over my life do I have? How do I handle the new responsibilities coming my way as an adult? How will I handle college (or my new job)? Is it okay if I'm stressed out?

Leg Three—Belonging: Where do I fit? What does this world have for me? What does God have for me? Where do family, friends, and dating fit? How important is it for me to connect to the local church?

My guess is you're already thinking about these questions and searching for your own answers. My hope is this book will help you consider who you are, why your choices matter, and what it means to belong to the family of God, giving you a stable base with strong legs to stand on as you head into the future.

The Goal of This Book

As you work through this book (but more importantly, as you work through this transition from adolescence to adulthood), I want to help you grow. So maybe I should let you know right from the start that I'm not a fabulous gardener. I wish I had a green thumb, but I don't. However, I do know a little about planting things. My family has done our share of landscaping over the years. I know you need the right things for plants and trees to grow. I know certain plants need to be in the shade and others need more sunlight. I know some plants need more water and others need hardly any water at all. But most of all I know God does the growing.

There are images of gardens and growth throughout the Bible. Scripture begins with Adam and Eve who walked in the garden of Eden in great fellowship with God until they made a decision to disobey him and eat fruit from the forbidden tree (Genesis 2–3). Jesus has an interesting connection to gardens too. He visited gardens throughout his life to pray. In fact, just hours before he died on the cross, he prayed in a garden asking his heavenly Father to sustain him (Matthew 26:36–46; Mark 14:32–42; Luke 22:39–46).

God cares a great deal about healthy growth. He wants you to grow in maturity, faith, obedience, health, wisdom, strength, and all other good things. So I'll play the part of the gardener by setting you up for growth with the right themes and questions. Your responsibility will be to partner with God in the process. Plant yourself in the right environment to be watered, fertilized, sunned, nurtured, and loved so you have the best shot at growing into a mature follower of Jesus. You can't always determine your environment, but as much as it depends on you, situate yourself so you can grow closer to Jesus as you make this transition. Helping you do that is the goal of this book.

> *I'm not really nervous, but I don't want to graduate and leave. I love high school. It has been an awesome experience that I don't want to end.*
>
> — Kurt, 17

You can use this book several different ways, one of which is reading it straight through. If you're a high school student, not everything will make sense yet, but don't worry; keep pressing on. Take the book with you as you journey to and through college. As different difficulties and situations arise, read it again.

You can also use this book as a reference guide or handbook, turning to the chapters (or specific issues) you need to deal with as you encounter them. Be sure to underline, circle, and highlight relevant passages so you have an ongoing reference list the next time an issue comes up. (You can write in the margins too! I won't tell.)

You can also share this book with your friends. Following Jesus is meant to be done in community, after all. You can use the questions at the end of each chapter to start discussions with your Jesus-following friends, as well as friends who don't know Jesus yet. Wrestle with the ideas and questions together. You might not agree with me at certain times — that's okay. Keep wrestling and pursuing Jesus as you make your transition into the real world. Aim for maturity, and God will help you get there.

Walking with Jesus isn't always easy, but you'll find the path brings growth, maturity, and life at its best. I'm so glad you've decided to join me on this journey!

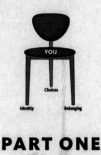

PART ONE

Identity — Who Am I?

I'm very excited about becoming an adult, and I look forward to the rest of my life with college and starting a family someday. There are some days I think about it, and I get really nervous. But I know whatever happens in my life is for a reason. God will take care of me and be there with me no matter what.

— Brittney, 17

The question "Who am I?" is probably driving you crazy by now. In the back of your mind or deep down in your heart, you're probably wondering what the answer is to this all-important question. When you get up in the morning and while you look in the mirror, get ready for school, eat breakfast, brush your teeth, drive to school, walk the halls, sit in class, go to work, and face every social situation you can think of, I bet this question pumps through your veins. Am I right?

Whether you're already out of high school or moving closer and closer to graduation, you may feel as though you should have it figured out by now. But the question remains: "Who am I *really*?" To make things worse, everyone else seems to know you better than you know yourself. They say, "That's not like you," and you think, *How do you know what's like me? How do you know who I am?*

The world may say your job, upbringing, family, or income defines you, but God says it's your relationship with him that truly defines who you are (Psalm 139:15–16). As you move through the next stages of your life, you'll develop a better understanding of what your identity is. And as you start that journey and become more independent of your parents upon leaving high school, I hope you become more dependent on God and a community of Jesus-followers in the context of a local church.

Discovering who you are is a bit like dancing. In this section, we'll explore some of the more challenging steps in that dance by looking at your story in Scripture, your belief in Jesus, your God-given design, and the role of doubts. Don't worry if you're not a good dancer. (I know I'm not!) This section will help you learn some of the basics. Before you know it, you'll be dancing like a pro.

CHAPTER 1

Grace: The Priceless Gift

I try to love God and love others. It is really hard sometimes.

— Billy, 16

The law detects, grace alone conquers sin.

— Saint Augustine of Hippo

Grace isn't a little prayer you chant before receiving a meal. It's a way to live.

— Jacqueline Winspear

The law tells me how crooked I am. Grace comes along and straightens me out.

— Dwight L. Moody

Real Freedom

Quick. What's the first thing that comes to mind when you hear the word *grace*? Is it a girl's name? A prayer before a meal? A characteristic of a person? Depending on your background, the word *grace* might be familiar or foreign. I want to start here because grace is often misunderstood, but it is possibly the most important piece of the puzzle of following Jesus beyond high school. Without grace there is no Christian faith, no Bible, no personal God, and no salvation. Life would not be worth living without this five-letter word, and the college experience will not be as fulfilling. There will be moments when you will need to receive grace from God and people, but also need to extend grace on the road to the real world.

Have you ever received something you didn't work for, earn, or deserve? Doing good things didn't get it for you. Acting a certain way didn't earn it. You didn't clean up your behavior for a day or a week to deserve it. It was just given to you with no strings attached.

Imagine a man convicted of a horrendous crime he didn't commit. He goes to the gallows completely innocent. Now imagine *you* are the one who committed the crime. He is innocent. You are guilty. He did nothing wrong. You did everything wrong. He didn't work for, earn, or deserve an ignominious death. You did.

In the Bible there is a verse that says, "For the wages of sin is death, but the gift of God is eternal life in Christ Jesus our Lord" (Romans 6:23). Because of our sin, we work for, earn, and therefore deserve spiritual death. In the story above, *you* deserved to be hung. But the verse doesn't end there. It says, *but*. What a wonderful little word. God gave us a gift. Like the innocent man in the story, someone else took your punishment for you. Jesus Christ provided the gift of eternal life for all who believe in him (Acts 16:31). It's free. Just believe.

This gift of Jesus Christ is salvation completely and totally without works or effort on our part. You can do nothing to get it. God didn't look at you and see goodness and therefore give you his Son. He saw guilty garbage piled up in your life. This is called sin, and grace is the only way to clean it up. It is God's determination to move before us. It started as God was making the world, and it continued after Adam and Eve sinned against him in the garden (Genesis 3). God's grace stretched throughout the Old Testament by way of Abraham, Isaac, Jacob, and Joseph, and on through Moses,

David, and the prophets. And it culminated in Jesus Christ on the cross, dying for our sins. We receive this grace by faith (Ephesians 2:8). Just believe in Jesus. That's it.

Have you heard the old song "Amazing Grace"? Here are some of the words written by the song's author, John Newton:

> Amazing Grace, how sweet the sound,
> That saved a wretch like me.
> I once was lost but now am found,
> Was blind, but now I see.
> T'was Grace that taught my heart to fear.
> And Grace, my fears relieved.
> How precious did that Grace appear
> The hour I first believed.
> Through many dangers, toils and snares
> I have already come;
> 'Tis Grace that brought me safe thus far
> And Grace will lead me home.

Maybe you've sung that hymn. Grace is amazing, but I think we've lost sight of some of its luster. This is why I'm starting here. If you've already received this grace and Jesus is your Savior, always remember how incredible God's grace really is. If you've been wrestling with God recently or for some time, maybe you need to take a closer look at his free favor given to you today. He loves you right where you are and not because you deserve it.

Grace is to capture, embrace, and love with no expectation of something in return.

I'm not really nervous, but I don't want to graduate and leave. I love high school. It has been an awesome experience that I don't want to end, though I am looking forward to learning even more about God as I head to college.

—Kurt, 17

God really did go ahead of you to show you incredible love through Christ's death on a cross. He is smiling in heaven for you. As a matter of fact, he is singing over you. *Really.* He's singing (see Zephaniah 3:17).

Paul's Perspective

Did you know that the opening lines of almost every one of Paul's letters to the churches mention grace? Yes, he starts with a prayer, but that isn't what I mean. Paul starts with the word *grace* because he got what grace is all about. In Romans he says, "To all in Rome who are loved by God and called to be his holy people: Grace and peace to you from God our Father and from the Lord Jesus Christ" (Romans 1:7). In 1 and 2 Corinthians, Galatians, Ephesians, Philippians, and 1 and 2 Thessalonians, Paul says in some variation, "grace and peace to you." In 1 and 2 Timothy, he gets really creative and changes the introduction to say, "grace, mercy and peace."

Even Jesus's most trusted friend, John, wrote his introduction in Revelation with "grace and peace to you" (Revelation 1:4). Grace was fully understood and was embraced as a hallmark in the New Testament because Jesus embodied grace. Grace is the point of the gospel.

Receive and Grow

Did you know you can grow in grace, not just receive it? Grace is not a once-and-for-all stagnant event. Grace is a now-and-forever dynamic relationship. You and I can get it and grow in it, even during the college years. Even Jesus had God's grace on him as he grew. When Jesus was a boy, Luke tells us "the child grew and became strong; he was filled with wisdom, and the grace of God was on him" (Luke 2:40).

God's desire is to give us more grace. We need to learn to rest and receive, not believing that we've somehow worked for it or earned it. More devotional time doesn't earn more grace from God. More time in prayer doesn't garner more grace. It was free when you embraced Jesus as Savior, and it continues to be free in the Christian life. Our God is a "forgiving God, gracious and compassionate, slow to anger and abounding in love" (Nehemiah 9:17). Did you notice the word *gracious?* Even in the Old Testament, God handed out unmerited favor that would eventually be complete in the cross of Christ.

Recently, I saw a saying on the side of a plumber's truck that read, "There is no place too dark, too deep, or too dirty that we are not willing to go." In that moment I thought of Jesus. He went to the darkest, deepest, dirtiest place for us, taking our sin on himself in order to extend his grace our way.

Extend

Now that you understand what grace is all about and you get that you can receive it and grow in it, are you able to extend grace to others? This is where the rubber meets the road as you make your way into the real world. Remember, grace is a piece of your identity in Christ. There will be friends, coworkers, classmates, roommates, and professors who make grace-giving easy, because you get along so well with them. There will also be those people who will make giving grace feel a whole lot harder to do. A friend burns you. Do you extend him grace? A professor doesn't seem to like you. Do you give a little grace? A roommate never cleans up her dirty clothes. Do you hand her a grace card?

Oftentimes there are a few hindrances to our extending grace to people. First, we have this tendency to compare ourselves to others. We look around to see if everyone else is acting, speaking, and dressing like us, and if they're listening to the same music and watching the same movies that we are. *If they aren't, they must be wrong*, we think. Christians can be the guiltiest of comparing and judging others based on minor issues of the faith. *Read that again.* Notice that I didn't say major issues but minor ones.

There are essentials of the faith worth dying for, but I'm talking about those gray areas—what songs we sing, where we pray, what translation of the Bible we read, and so on. We seem to have this desire for all Christians to look alike, sound alike, and act alike; but our God is creative, and he didn't make us all the same.

Second, we're hindered in extending grace because of our tendency to control. Every now and then I read the comics. Do you remember *Peanuts* with Charlie Brown? I saw one strip recently where Linus is sitting alone watching television. In storms Lucy demanding that he change the channel to the one she wants to watch. Rather meekly he asks, "What makes you think you can walk in and take over?" She blurts out, "These five fingers!", which she has tightened into a fist. It works. As she assumes control, Linus slips out of the room. He then looks at his own five fingers and asks, "Why can't you guys get organized like that?"

There are lots of "Lucys" in the world who want it all to revolve around them. You will run into people who want to tell everyone else what to do and how to do it, and if you don't file in accordingly, something bad is going to happen. It's hard to give grace to people like that. They don't deserve it, right? But that's why we get the honor of giving grace just like Jesus did for us. It's hard to show grace when we feel manipulated and abused, but remember the love Jesus showed us: "While we were still sinners, Christ died for us" (Romans 5:8). Instead of withdrawing like Linus when you don't feel loved or appreciated, extend grace like Jesus.

Grace Gives

As you make your way into new relationships and the exciting journey into the unknown, receive grace, grow in grace, and extend grace. Here are some tips for the journey. In front of and behind others' backs, speak words that are intended to build up, not bring down. Be selfless and focus on the needs of others above your own needs. Forgive an offense quickly and freely. Don't hold a grudge. Swallow your pride and say to everyone, "I'm sorry," "I was wrong," and "Please forgive me." Live your life with the goal of no regrets. Don't keep a "Kindness Score" with your roommate. Never give up on people just because they made a mistake. If you need perspective, look in the mirror and then look at the cross of Christ. Show people mercy when they don't deserve it. Finally, read 1 Corinthians 13 regularly so that your love is pure.

God's grace for you really is amazing. The more we know him, the more grace we have to give away. You will be blessed in this next chapter of your life if you do.

Questions for the Journey

1. What does grace mean to you?
2. Have you received the grace of God in Jesus Christ by making him your Savior?
3. How can you grow in grace during these transitional years?
4. What is the hardest part about getting, giving, and growing in grace?
5. Who could you extend more grace to this week?

CHAPTER 2

The Bible: Your Authority

God is the Word and the Word is God. If I want to be closer to him, I have to listen to what he's telling me. No relationship has ever worked when one person spoke and the other always chose not to listen, so how can my relationship with God work if I choose not to listen to him?

—Shae, 18

All Scripture is God-breathed and is useful for teaching, rebuking, correcting and training in righteousness, so that the servant of God may be thoroughly equipped for every good work.

—2 Timothy 3:16 – 17

A Good Narrative

We're all drawn to a good story, aren't we? Stories are fun. But what is it about a story that brings us in, grabs hold of us, and doesn't let go until there's some sort of resolution?

My uncle is a master storyteller. For as long as I can remember, Uncle Deane has told stories and jokes in dramatic fashion. He draws you in with his gestures and engages you with his theatrics and vocal inflections. The golf course is one of his favorite places to tell stories. We could probably finish a round of golf a few hours earlier if it weren't for his tales, but they're worth every minute.

In *The Living Reminder*, author Henri Nouwen talks about the power of stories: We can dwell in a story, walk around, and find our own place. The story confronts but does not oppress; the story inspires but does not manipulate. The story invites us to an encounter, a dialog, a mutual sharing. A story that guides is a story that opens a door and offers us space in which to search and boundaries to help us find what we seek.[1]

> *I study Scripture every night: sometimes for hours, sometimes just a page before I fall asleep. At times it's monotonous, but oftentimes God shows me some gem I'd never seen or realized before and it changes my life. Without these insights, I'd be lost.*
>
> —David, 18

Stories connect with the deepest longings inside of us because they resonate with the journey each one of us takes as we grow and change and experience the world throughout our lives—our own stories. And our individual tales are all intimately connected, coming together to form a divine tapestry—a single, great big human story.

When interviewing for various jobs, I've often been asked some form of the question, "What's your story?" Those interviewers wanted to know where I came from and what makes me tick. They wanted to know what was important to me and how my passions, gifts, and abilities drove me to action.

Similarly, in the college and post-college ministries I've led, we ask the attendees to share their stories every week—not just their testimonies about when they came to know Jesus, but their current stories. We want to know what they're learning about life and God. We're interested in authentic connection. We long to know—really know—one another. By sharing stories, our community members learn what

---

[1] Henri J. M. Nouwen, *The Living Reminder: Service and Prayer in Memory of Jesus Christ* (New York: HarperCollins, 1977), 66.

drives one another, what we're currently learning, and what our common struggles are. This is inspiring. This is divine tapestry.

So what's your story? Spend some time right now thinking about your past. Consider the great joys of your life as well as the hard times God has led you through. If you know Jesus, think of how you came to know him. Ponder how God directed you to the place you are today. Celebrate his guiding grace as we begin to consider how all of our stories connect.

Our stories connect to one another's, but they also connect to the larger story of God's work in our world. It's a grand narrative in which God weaves the stories of every human on his earth into an intricate depiction of his glory.

The psalmist in the Old Testament says:

> For you created my inmost being;
> you knit me together in my mother's womb.
> I praise you because I am fearfully and wonderfully made;
> your works are wonderful,
> I know that full well.
> My frame was not hidden from you
> when I was made in the secret place,
> when I was woven together in the depths of the earth.
> Your eyes saw my unformed body;
> all the days ordained for me were written in your book
> before one of them came to be.
>
> Psalm 139:13–16

You see? Your story is connected to something greater.

Dog Bones

Have you ever watched a dog with a bone? My dog, Mocha, loves bones. Each bone is her prize, and she protects it at all costs. She growls playfully, a low rumble expressing her delight. When she's done gnawing on a bone, she licks her chops and paws. And bones aren't her only joy: She's also been known to put her front paws on the counter, snatch a loaf of bread, and devour it. One time we thought she'd eaten a whole bag of bagels, only to discover she'd buried them in our couches and chairs for later!

> *I've just started reading Scripture. I feel closer to Jesus than ever before.*
>
> — Kurt, 17

As I was studying Scripture one day, I found a verse that compares God to "a great lion" growling over its prey (Isaiah 31:4). I thought of Mocha growling over her bone. This is when it gets really fun. The Hebrew word for growl is *hagah*. Say it out loud: *hagah*. It's a fun word that can also mean "to meditate." So Mocha—with these low growls of enjoyment and playful delight over her bone—is meditating over her prize.

Scripture uses *hagah* in other ways too. The very first Psalm says the person is blessed "whose delight is in the law of the LORD, and who meditates on his law day and night" (Psalm 1:2). The psalmist says he thinks about God on his bed at night (Psalm 63:6). He dwells on God. The word *hagah* was used by the Jews for reading, studying, meditating, and apparently for growling. With *hagah* we use our teeth, tongue, taste buds, stomach, and intestines for chewing, swallowing, and digesting. With *hagah* we understand God is good: "Taste and see that the LORD is good" (Psalm 34:8).

What happens as we truly meditate on the stories of Scripture? We find them to be alive with meaning for us today. We discover more and more ways in which the pieces of our stories intersect with God's story. This is a *hagah* moment.[2]

Directional Dysfunction

I have a problem, and I'm willing to admit it: I'm terrible with directions. If there is a disease characterized by frequent disorientation,

---

[2] Eugene Peterson inspired my study of the Hebrew word *hagah* in his book *Eat This Book: A Conversation in the Art of Spiritual Reading* (Eerdmans, 2006).

I'm pretty sure I've got it. As a matter of fact, I think I'll start a recovery group called ADD (not that kind, although I might have that disorder too)—All-Direction Dysfunctional.

How are you with directions? How's your internal compass? Have you ever been to a new place and didn't have a clue where anything was?

When my wife Laurie and I moved to Littleton, Colorado, we didn't know where anything was located. We didn't know street names. We didn't know where anyone lived. We didn't know where our church was in relation to everywhere else. We couldn't find a Walmart or a Target. We didn't know how to find the zoo, where to get an oil change, or where to find a dentist or hospital. And most critically, we couldn't find the nearest Starbucks or the Barnes and Noble! Thank goodness for those mountains in the west—at least I knew where they were (until it got dark)!

So what do you think we did to learn where things were located in Littleton? Do you think we sat down with a map and memorized where every street was located? That would never work for me. We learned as we lived. We kept our eyes open. We asked questions. We looked at MapQuest (a lot). We went for drives to look around— especially to find a home. When we visited a new location, we paid attention. We started to observe the same places, and eventually we found Starbucks, Target, and the nearest gas station. We discovered where people lived in relation to one another. Before long, we had a pretty good grasp of where to go and how to get there.

When it comes to studying Scripture, many of us feel the same way. We feel lost. We know a few landmark stories, but we have no idea how all of these little stories fit into the larger, God-sized story. And we don't know how our own personal stories are a part of God's story either. So as we study Scripture, we need to discover as we go.

A friend of mine once said, "You can't steer a parked car." In a similar way, you won't learn how your story fits with God's story unless you open God's Word and start reading. As you travel further into Scripture, you'll discover connections. You'll begin to remember other, similar places. You'll begin to think to yourself, *Oh, I get it. The sacrifices they talk about in the Old Testament are connected to Jesus being the last and most important sacrifice for me.* The stories will begin to connect—both with each other and with your life.

As you read the stories of Scripture, try to experience them in your imagination. Try to picture yourself visiting the Sea of Galilee and listening to Jesus teach. What does the water look like as it laps against the shore? What does Jesus's voice sound like? How does the sand feel between your toes? As you travel through the various passages, look for landmarks—key people, places, and events. These landmarks can help guide you to the main story just as the picture on a puzzle box helps you see where the pieces fit. You might find it helpful to read summaries of various books of the Bible as a way of grasping the bigger story. Or you may want to slow down and learn one location at a time by focusing on a particular character, theme, or book within Scripture. Glimpsing the big picture and then slowing down to enjoy the view is important.

Glancers and Gazers

A few summers ago, I led a team of high school students on a two-week leadership-experience trip in Europe. On the last day, we hung out in Paris. (It was awesome!) Of course, a few of us went to the Louvre, the famous art museum that houses the *Mona Lisa* and many other well-known paintings.

The Louvre is made up of eight departments that display 35,000 works in 60,000 square meters of exhibition space. It's huge. After an hour or two of looking around, I needed a break. And I did what many people do during a break in a public space: I people watched.

As I observed thousands of people coming and going, I noticed there were two types: glancers and gazers. The glancers appeared to be trying to see every piece of art in the Louvre within a few hours, which is impossible. Even if you looked at each piece for just a minute, you'd need three weeks to see them all. But these glancers

> *I need Scripture! It has become my addiction. I don't even think I do it right, but God is teaching me every day.*
>
> — Annie, 29

still did their best to see everything, and they never spent too much time on any one piece of art.

Then there were the gazers — the students of history, art, and culture. They'd stop at one painting, look at it from every angle, notice the fine details, take pictures, and write notes in their journals. A gazer might spend an hour in front of a single piece of art before moving on to the next.

In the same way, I've noticed two types of Scripture students. Glancers read the Bible quickly, but they don't take the time to understand how all the stories fit together. They seem primarily focused on "getting it done." Meanwhile, gazers take their time by reading and studying, seeking to understand how God's story intersects with their own stories. Gazers long to fall in love with God more deeply.

There's a big difference between reading Scripture and studying it. Thomas à Kempis once said, "Do not read the Scriptures to satisfy curiosity or to pass the time, but study such things as to move your heart to devotion." Let the greater story work on you.

Ezra was a gazer who did exactly that. He was a man after God's heart who loved to study God's Word. Ezra and the Israelites were exiled to Babylon after King Nebuchadnezzar and his army ransacked Jerusalem. Many years later, after God softened the heart of King Artaxerxes (a king who ruled over Babylon and the exiles almost a hundred years after Nebuchadnezzar), the Israelites returned to their homeland. Ezra tells the story of the Israelites' return to Jerusalem in Ezra 6–7.

Ezra journeyed from Babylon to Jerusalem with thousands of other Jews. The Bible tells us Ezra was a teacher "well versed in the Law of Moses" (Ezra 7:6). King Artaxerxes granted him return because "the hand of the LORD his God was on him" (7:6). But why was God's hand on him? Because Ezra "devoted himself to the study and observance of the Law of the LORD, and to teaching its decrees and laws in Israel" (7:10). I love that! Ezra was devoted to studying the law of God. And he didn't just read God's Word; he lived it. He taught it to others. Ezra is just one model of someone who lived and loved Scripture.

Heading Out the Door with Scripture Under Your Arm

In one of his letters to Timothy, Paul wrote, "All Scripture is God-breathed and is useful for teaching, rebuking, correcting and training in righteousness, so that the servant of God may be thoroughly equipped for every good work" (2 Timothy 3:16–17). Did you catch what Paul says is the purpose of Scripture? To equip you. It equips you for the real world you're entering. It equips you with God's wisdom. It helps you understand that your story, your journey is connected to the stories of so many others who've gone before you. It helps you look back so you can move forward in faith.

The author of the book of Hebrews says, "Remember your leaders, who spoke the word of God to you. Consider the outcome of their way of life and imitate their faith. Jesus Christ is the same yesterday and today and forever" (13:7–8). We have such a legacy to live; so many have gone before us.

So why do we have such a hard time reading and studying the connecting story our Creator has given us? Why don't we see Scripture as a filet mignon ready to be devoured? Why don't we savor it, meditate on it, *hagah* it the way my dog loves her bone?

I believe one reason is we don't really believe it gives us life. Even if we'd never say it out loud, we often think of the Bible as a dead book. We think it's just a collection of stories from the distant past. We don't see it as being alive.

But it *is* alive. It laughs with you, cries with you, and serves as a mirror and compass for your life. Your identity is revealed as you devour the stories of Scripture.

Some people eat and drink too fast. My five-year-old son loves to drink hot cocoa. Every time Levi is given a cup of cocoa, he drinks it in one gulp. He doesn't even put the cup down. One gulp. Gone.

Many study Scripture this way, going at it quickly. We need to slow down with Scripture—tasting, chewing, savoring, swallowing, and digesting it. We need to take these God-breathed words to heart and open ourselves to change—and transformation. The Bible is your lifeline, your life source. It's your identity in God. It's food for the soul.

Will you really get into reading and studying Scripture? Will you find your own story in God's story? It's your food. Your whole life after high school depends on it. Go *hagah*!

QUESTIONS FOR THE JOURNEY

1. On a scale of 1 to 10 (with 10 being "I love it") how much do you enjoy reading the Bible?

2. How could you grow in your desire to study Scripture?

3. Do you see Scripture as just another book or as a living, breathing companion? What difference do you think this makes in your motivation to read and study it?

4. What can you do this week to improve your Scripture study?

CHAPTER 3

The Bible: The Whole Story

Most people are bothered by those passages in Scripture which they cannot understand; but as for me, I always noticed that the passages in Scripture which trouble me most are those which I do understand.

— Mark Twain

I did not go through the Bible. The Bible went through me.

— A. W. Tozer

Big Picture

God is in control. Have you heard that phrase before? Maybe you've thought it or said it from time to time as a reassurance that he is indeed sovereign. I have. I've needed to. When difficulty comes your way, having an anchor to keep the boat from flipping over in the storm is important.

But have you said "God is in control" when life is going well— things seem to be working out, prayers seem to be heard, and your life seems to be lining up according to plan? Maybe you've rejoiced at the goodness of God's perfect plan in recent days. Whether we're currently struggling, in need of a place to hold tight, or jumping up and down and praising God, we need to be reminded that God's hand is orchestrating a perfect plan that is coming to a culmination for all of the heavens and earth.

I wanted to include a chapter that offers a quick look at the story of the Bible. For many of you, this will be review, but for others this will be new. Maybe you've just come to know Jesus as Savior, or maybe you're new to the stories and characters in the Bible. I do promise that no matter what your faith level, this overview will provide a fresh perspective for you to hang on to and grow from for years to come. It is lengthy but well worth the high-altitude view. So grab your Bible and get ready to look up some verses. Let me tell you the sovereign story of the Bible that leads up to your life today—because you are one of the characters in the story of God.

Act One: The Heart of God in Genesis

All of history is part of one sovereign, divine tapestry woven by the hand of God. Sometimes it is hard to see why things happened in the Bible or in modern history, like looking at the back of a woven cloth. But when you step back and flip the tapestry over, it becomes apparent that God is in control and his plan is beautiful. Our place in his "cloth" may not become evident until we've gained a new and broader perspective, and many times allowed more time to pass, but when we take a look at the whole of the Bible from Genesis to Revelation, it helps us see how each thread adds shading and shape to the image God weaves.

God Begins His Quest

Did you know that from the beginning of God's creation of and inter-action with humans, he demonstrated his compassionate desire to be in relationship with us? From the very moment sin entered the world through the disobedience of Adam and Eve, God began to pursue us with his grace. (If you haven't already, read over chapter one.) Immediately after Adam and Eve ate the fruit from the tree, God reached out by saying, "Where are you?" He loved his creation, and he loved his people. He wasn't about to give up on them (Genesis 3:8, 9, 15). Theologians call this the "Adamic Covenant," as in Genesis 3:15 God extends his far-reaching grace and hints at redemption through Jesus Christ on the cross. God pursues people with passion immediately following the fall!

God's Purposes

When I was in college, I struggled with Spanish class. I was so nervous trying to learn a foreign language that I felt sick most of the time. A new language just wasn't in my DNA. Oftentimes Christians view language and diversity of culture as major obstacles to the world's coming to know Christ. Yes, culture and language do bring logistical challenges to those sharing Christ, but they come from the compassionate heart of God and actually assist in the process of reaching the world for Christ. Maybe you don't believe me. Let's take a look at the passage describing the birth of the nations as distinct people groups with their own languages and cultures (Genesis 11:1–9).

Why did God divide the languages of the world and give birth to the nations? First, man was sinful, evil, and wicked. God grieved this fact and longed for a relationship to be restored with him (Genesis 6:5–8). After people began walking away from that relationship again after the flood, God knew that nothing would stop the evil of these people from growing, because they spoke the same language. He needed to stop them from pursuing depravity (Genesis 11:5–7). As a result, Paul shares with us in the book of Acts that it

> *The Bible is the record of what God said and did in history, so it has to be a priority for us to study it and be familiar with it. It's through the Bible that we see how Jesus treated people, showed love, and approached the world. Without it, we're not going to be able to grow much at all.*
>
> *— Adam, 23*

was part of God's plan to separate these evil people by dividing up their languages and scattering them over the earth. Why did God do this? So that people would seek him, find him, and be back in a right relationship with him (Acts 17:24–27).

I have three wonderful children, but sometimes the only way to stop the madness in the house is to send them to their rooms for a few minutes so they can come to their senses and regain right relationship with one another and with me. God did something similar—separating and forcing the people to reflect—when he made it difficult for them to communicate with each other. Now without the great might of their former civilization, and being unable to coordinate their efforts with one another, they had new and overwhelming reasons to seek him. As a result, the plan God initiated at the Tower of Babel was proactive and redemptive, not reactive and punitive. It's really an amazing strategy set in motion because of God's love for people.

All Nations Blessed

In the chapter directly after his division of the nations into cultural and linguistic groups, God chooses one man with whom to establish his covenant and promises Abraham that "all peoples on earth will be blessed through you" (Genesis 12:3). This promise, or the Abrahamic covenant, can be divided into two parts, the top line and the bottom line (Genesis 12:2). The top line says (and I paraphrase), "I will bless you by making your descendants into a great nation." The bottom line says, "I will make you a great man so you will be a blessing." God was setting up his plan to reach the world through a person who would turn into a people.

The Covenant Confirmed

After settling in the land of Canaan, Abraham struggled with God's promise. After all, he was getting up there in years, and he still had no children. So he asked God for some surety. Take a moment to read the amazing account of God's confirmation of the covenant in Genesis 15. In that culture, two people making a covenant used the lifeblood of animals to demonstrate their commitment. As Abraham sleeps, he sees a vision of God in the form of fire passing through the slaughtered and separated animals, thereby promising, with symbolism relevant to Abraham, to fulfill his covenant to bless the nations through Abraham.

More Covenant Confirmation

God continued to confirm his covenant with Abraham and Abraham's offspring, giving special consideration to the bottom line, "so you will be a blessing." The covenant was confirmed again with Abraham in Genesis 18:18 and 22:17–18. Isaac, Jacob, and Joseph all get affirmation later in the book of Genesis (26:2–4; 28:10–14; 50:24–25).

So why all the reminders? Because we forget. We're human. We doubt and lose faith. But we don't have to worry about God coming through for us. When he makes a promise, he keeps it.

I will never forget buying my old VW Jetta years ago. I met the seller at my bank so he could cash the check. We met, shook hands, and he walked into the bank. I knew the money was in my account, but I was still nervous that something would go wrong, preventing my taking ownership of the car. Unlike with human promises, when God makes a promise, we don't need to be nervous that it won't come to pass. It was true for Abraham, and it's true for you as you make this transition from high school into college and beyond.

Fast-Forward into the Future

God's redeeming plan was now in place, but the full measure of the top line of the Abrahamic covenant would not be fulfilled for years to come. Through his graciousness, God allowed Abraham and his descendants a rare perspective on the timing of God's redeeming promise. In Genesis 15, God cracks open the door to the future, allowing his chosen man to see just what was going to happen and when.

> Then the LORD said to him, "Know for certain that for four hundred years your descendants will be strangers in a country not their own and that they will be enslaved and mistreated there. But I will punish the nation they serve as slaves, and afterward they will come out with great possessions. You, however, will go to your ancestors in peace and be buried at a good old age. In the fourth generation your descendants will come back here, for the sin of the Amorites has not yet reached its full measure."
>
> Genesis 15:13 – 16

Abraham was allowed to see *way* into the future. His descendants would remain in slavery for four hundred years, longing to be freed, wondering where God was and why he was waiting to deliver them. But in his time, God would be faithful to rescue them. God even promised that Abraham would live a long life and die in old age. The Bible records that all of these promises came true. God can be trusted. He is on a pursuit to rescue the world from sin—even in the book of Genesis.

Act Two: The Heart of God in the Rest of the Old Testament

Let's pick up speed. You can trust God! When he makes a promise, nothing can keep him from bringing it to pass for "there is no wisdom, no insight, no plan that can succeed against the LORD" (Proverbs 21:30). God is willing to perform incredible miracles in order to bring the top line of the Abrahamic covenant to pass.

God Remembers His Covenant

Just as God told Abraham, the people of Israel were enslaved by Egypt for more than four hundred years. But God didn't forget his covenant with Abraham (Exodus 2:23 – 25). Can you imagine waiting four hundred years for this promise to come to pass? Some say we are the impatient and entitled generation. We want our food fast, and we expect it to be value sized. We need our computers to be faster and faster. And as if cell phone calls weren't fast enough, we now have texting. Can you imagine the world before texting? How did we live? (Did you catch my sarcasm?)

> *When I study Scripture, I feel like I can conquer anything. But sometimes it's hard to stay consistent in your walk with God.*
>
> — Rachel, 15

God's promises are true, but sometimes we need to wait for them to come to fulfillment. The Israelites waited for four hundred years (that's more than four generations), and they weren't hanging around some plush spa either. They endured persecuting slavery.

A Nation Founded

Following their miraculous deliverance from Egypt, the Israelites gathered at the base of Mount Sinai to receive instructions from God through Moses. This was God's first specific communication with his people *as a nation*. It's similar to the American Declaration of Independence in that God explains why he made them a nation and what their purpose will be (Exodus 19:3–6).

After making it clear that he's chosen Israel to be his holy nation, God goes on to give them an explanation of how to live in a manner pleasing to him. The next chapter in the Bible outlines the rules for holy living (Exodus 20), or better known as the Ten Commandments. The first five are helpful for the Israelites' vertical relationship with God, and the next five speak to their horizontal relationships with one another.

Fast-forward many years to Jesus's reply when asked what the greatest commandment is. He responded, " 'Love the Lord your God with all your heart and with all your soul and with all your mind.' This is the first and greatest commandment. And the second is like it: 'Love your neighbor as yourself.' All the Law and the Prophets hang on these two commandments" (Matthew 22:37–40). All of the commandments from Exodus 20 and all the prophets have said would be "hung" on Jesus's commandment because it's the fulfillment of the heart of God.

Israel's Failure

Although God went to great lengths to implement his plan, it wouldn't take long for the people of Israel to become impatient and turn away from his purposes (Exodus 32:25–29). In the midst of the nation's disobedience, God sends Moses to issue an "altar call" straight from him. In response, the Levites rallied to God. It was God's desire for the whole of Israel to return in commitment to God, but it seems the Levites (three thousand in number, per Genesis 32:28) were ready to go with God. Oh, how we do the same thing. Have you ever been in the same place as these Levites? Disobeying. Confessing. Recommitting. I am so grateful God is a relentless God, pursuing me with his love at all costs. Aren't you?

From Nation to Tribe

Let's be reminded that God clearly stated that his original plan was to raise up a whole nation of "priests" who would mediate his covenant blessings to all the families of the earth (Exodus 19:5–6). This plan was initiated at the time of the Passover in Egypt, but later modified due to the disobedience of Israel at Mount Sinai (Numbers 3; 8:16–19). God's original plan was always to have a lot of people sharing his love with the whole world. He wasn't interested in having just a few paid professionals doing all the work, but the whole nation of Israel sharing the good news of God's greatness.

Consider Peter's words, spoken centuries later: "But you are a chosen people, a royal priesthood, a holy nation, God's special possession, that you may declare the praises of him who called you out of darkness into his wonderful light" (1 Peter 2:9). Today, you are chosen, royal, holy, and special. Go show his light to a dark world. This is your greatest purpose as you make your way out of high school and into the world.

Proactive Promises with a Reactive People

God's intention was for his holy nation to fulfill the bottom line of the Abrahamic covenant: "you will be a blessing" to "all peoples on earth." As a nation of priests, they were to share the blessings of their special covenant relationship with all the peoples of the earth. Yet at the highest point of their history, they were reactive rather than proactive with regard to God's purpose. Hidden away in the book of Leviticus is an interesting picture of the heart of God. Take a look at how God feels about those on the outside of the nation of Israel.

> The foreigner residing among you must be treated as your native-born. Love them as yourself, for you were foreigners in Egypt. I am the LORD your God.
>
> Leviticus 19:34

God's heart's desire all along—and even now—has been for the "foreigner" to be invited in. He wants his name to be recognized and proclaimed so all peoples can know him and love him. The people of Israel were told to serve the foreigner for the purpose of redemption. Sometimes God is represented in the Old Testament as an angry God; but in fact, he is a compassionate and loving God who longs for all people to know him. He is doing the same today.

Remnant Remembered

In spite of the fact that the nation of Israel failed to live out the fullness of God's plan for them, he raised up a remnant to remind them of their shortcomings and to clarify for us his unwavering commitment to bless all the peoples of the earth. Multiple psalms point to the heart of God for the nations, starting in our own neighborhoods (Psalm 2:8–12; Psalm 46:10; Psalm 67; Psalm 96:3; Psalm 99:2; Psalm 113:4).

What the Bible Can Do

Pierce the heart, convict of sin (Hebrews 4:12)

Regenerate and transform a life (1 Peter 1:23)

Produce a living faith in God (Romans 10:17)

Cleanse and purify a person's heart and life (Psalm 119:9 – 11)

Protect from heresy and error (Acts 20:29 – 32)

Bring joy and rejoicing to the heart (Jeremiah 15:16)

Speak peace to the troubled soul (Psalm 85:8)

Make us wiser than our teachers (Psalm 119:99)

Testify about Jesus (John 5:39)

Help us in many practical ways (2 Timothy 3:16)

Act Three: The Heart of God in the New Testament

This brings us to the New Testament, where God's redemption plan continues. Unfortunately, there is a common misunderstanding among Christians when it comes to the concept of God's heart for redeeming all people. Many believers think the biblical concept of redemption starts with the Great Commission of Matthew 28. But Jesus came not to *introduce* the redemptive heart of God, but rather to *fulfill* the promise God made to Adam in Genesis 3 and now Abraham that through his offspring all peoples on earth would be blessed. Let's move on to the New Testament and see God's desire to redeem people.

The Example of Jesus's Life

Throughout Jesus's life on earth, he modeled and taught on the redemptive heart of God through his ministry and mandates to

his disciples. His words and works demonstrated the thinking of God because he is
God. This didn't just *conclude* Jesus's ministry; it *included* all he did on earth. Let's look
at the examples of redemption Jesus lays out for us.

> *Jesus is my rock and shield.*
>
> —David, 18

In John's gospel, Jesus goes out of his way to travel by way of Samaria to have an encounter with a Samaritan woman (John 4:1–42). Jesus broke two cultural rules when he met with this woman. First, he was alone with her. A Jewish man did not meet with a woman alone or speak to a woman unless she was his wife. Second, Jesus spent time with and spoke to a Samaritan. Jews did not associate with Samaritans because they considered them to be half-breeds who followed a corrupted theology and therefore were considered unclean.

Jesus uses a water metaphor to share who he is with the woman hauling water from the well. He points out her "indiscretion" in being married several times, but he still introduces her to "living water." She would never have to go searching for love and fulfillment in the wrong ways again if she'd only believe in Jesus. His compassionate heart and redemptive message—to a woman he shouldn't even be talking to—was extraordinary. It caused the woman to share this news with her village, asking, "Could this be the Messiah?" (John 4:29). God goes to extreme measures to take his redemptive gospel to another people group, the Samaritans.

Jesus was concerned with taking the gospel to not only the Samaritans, but to all people. Over and over again throughout the Gospels (Matthew, Mark, Luke, and John), Jesus declares that he is the answer to their sin problem. He is "the way and the truth and the life. No one comes to the Father except through [him]" (John 14:6).

The Commissioning

On three separate occasions following his resurrection, the famous last words of Jesus are recorded. Maybe you've heard of them. The responsibility of the disciples to reach all people in order to fulfill the heart of God was at hand. The baton of God's relay race was passed from Jesus to his disciples.

First, in the upper room after the resurrection, Jesus shares with his disciples that his name will be preached to all the nations (Luke 24:45–47).

Second, on the mountain of Galilee after Jesus rose from the dead, his most famous commissioning service took place (Matthew 28:16–20). Jesus emphasizes the all-inclusiveness of God's redemption by using phrases like *all authority, all nations, obey everything,* and *with [his disciples] always.* Jesus's encounter with his disciples in Galilee prior to the ascension was distinct for at least two reasons. First, Jesus announced this meeting ahead of time. He alerted the disciples several times, telling them where and when to meet (Matthew 26:32; 28:7; 28:16). Second, it was the largest crowd to whom Jesus gave his final instructions. More than five hundred were present (1 Corinthians 15:6). Redemption is for the whole world.

Third, Luke records in Acts 1 that Jesus tells his apostles that the Holy Spirit will give them power to be his witnesses "in all Judea and Samaria, and to the ends of the earth" (1:8).

Act Four: The Heart of God at the Beginning of the Church

Following the ascension of Jesus and the descent of the Holy Spirit at Pentecost, the New Testament church experienced explosive numerical growth. Even though the church was growing because of God's grace, these early Christians struggled with their responsibility to take the gospel to the ends of the earth. Immediately following the commissioning of the disciples, they find themselves back in their home base, the upper room, wondering what to do next (Acts 1:12–14). What would it take for the New Testament church to accept the role of sharing God's redemptive plan with the Gentile world?

I don't know about you, but I find myself in the same spot sometimes. I know Jesus has come. I believe in him, but I'm still stifled and don't communicate the gospel to an unbelieving world like I should. Maybe you can relate. Maybe you need a worldview shift like Peter's.

Reshaping Peter's Worldview

Peter quickly rose to the surface as the undisputed leader of the early church. Yet he had been taught to follow a worldview that focused only on the Jewish people. He accepted that false worldview without realizing it was in direct conflict with God's plan to reach all the nations. (Take a look at chapter 8 on worldviews right now, if you have time.)

Acts 10 recounts God's plan to expose the un-Christian parts of Peter's worldview and begin the process of mobilizing the early church for reaching the world for Jesus. Basically, Peter had a supernatural confrontation with God. First, there was a supernatural revelation in which God showed Peter that his worldview was off base and God's desire was for the gospel to go to all people (Acts 10:9–16). Next, there was a supernatural invitation for Peter to take the gospel to a Gentile (Acts 10:17–23). Finally, there was a supernatural reception where Peter finally got it and immediately took the gospel to an important but spiritually lost man named Cornelius who'd also been contacted by God. While at Cornelius's house, Peter led many Gentiles to a saving belief in Jesus (Acts 10:24–48).

Confrontation in Jerusalem

We might assume that the religious leaders in Jerusalem would be overjoyed to hear of the conversion of Cornelius and his household. But they were so consumed by their own worldview, they couldn't see the hand of God at work (Acts 11:2).

We do the same thing. We get stuck in our own Christian bubbles thinking there's only one way to share the gospel with only one group of people. The message of the gospel remains the same, but the methods and extent of the gospel is for all different peoples everywhere.

New Testament Missions

God's promise to bless all the nations is coming to pass. In Acts 8 we see the sovereign hand of God at work in setting the stage for New Testament missions. The heartbeat of God's plan is still to reach the whole world with the gospel.

God even gives us a strategy to "get the Word out." The plan was to begin in Jerusalem, move on to Judea and Samaria, and finally reach out to the ends of the earth (Acts 1:8). The rest of the book of Acts shows God using people to take the gospel far and wide. Acts 1–7 covers the mission in Jerusalem, Acts 8–10 the mission in Judea and Samaria, and Acts 11–28 the journey of the gospel to the ends of the earth.

As the good news of Jesus's life, death, and resurrection moves out, the first sending church (a church with a missions outreach) to the Gentile world is established in a city named Antioch. Does your church sponsor missionaries somewhere in the world? If so, your church is part of a long line of life-giving churches that began with the church in Antioch that sent Paul out into the world for his three missionary journeys.

The Revelation of the Church and Today

Through the death of Jesus Christ on the cross, God opened the door to the Gentile world and gave birth to a new people. All people who believe in Jesus as their Rescuer or Savior have been made right with God. This means you have been "credited with righteousness based on faith" (Romans 4:16–25; Galatians 3:6–9; 1 Peter 2:4–10; Revelation 5:9–10).

Therefore, believers in Jesus everywhere have been commissioned by God to accept the high challenge of extending his blessing to all the peoples of the earth in fulfillment of his covenant with Abraham. At the same time, God is not done with the physical Israel. There are many prophecies yet to be fulfilled.

Today, as you make your way from high school into college and beyond, you have an awesome responsibility to partner with God to take his redemptive plan of salvation to your friends, roommates, professors, family members, neighbors, and coworkers. It is the plan God initiated in Genesis 3 after Adam and Eve blew it, and it will extend until Jesus comes back to take the church home, setting up his full kingdom reign. Will you take the joyful honor of embracing the good news and sharing it with others?

QUESTIONS FOR THE JOURNEY

1. Have you ever thought of the Bible as the story of God's pursuit of humankind?

2. What parts of the story did you already know? What was new for you?

3. How does seeing God as a "loving Rescuer" change your perspective? Do you see him pursuing people today? Why? How?

4. How can this summary help you in your daily relationship with God?

CHAPTER 4

Belief: Faith in Jesus

Jesus is loving, caring, and awesome. He was the ultimate sacrifice. Following Christ is like resting in our identity with him.

—Annabel, 15

Now faith is confidence in what we hope for and assurance about what we do not see.

—Hebrews 11:1

Custom Shading

Several summers ago, I was invited to speak at a youth-and-family camp in Pennsylvania. It was right in the middle of July, and it was brutally humid. In the mornings and early afternoons, we'd gather, and I'd encourage and challenge the students from Scripture. By the end of the afternoon session, not only were the students ready for a break, but I was ready for some games in the great outdoors as well. When I speak at camps, I always try to get involved in the fun stuff too. I have no problem "suffering" for Jesus.

As you might imagine, we played a variety of games—including a few anything-goes, full-contact ones. They were unbelievably fun, but also a little dangerous. You know the kind.

One afternoon, someone pulled out the water balloon launcher.

All of the youth campers gathered in a pack on one end of the field as the counselors launched the balloons forty-some yards toward the group. Whoever caught the balloon shrapnel in the air got big points. Whoever got the most points was the winner. Easy, right?

> *I would describe Jesus as the perfect gift from heaven and role model to follow. Jesus is our Lord and Savior. He showed us how to live.*
>
> —Rachel, 15

It sounded fun, so I joined in the action. As the balloons came in, the most athletic, competitive, die-hard guys seemed to take over. Not wanting to be outdone, I jumped in with the rest of them and did my best to collect parts of balloons. Then—BOOM! I came down on top of one of the high school guys. To be precise, my top row of teeth came down on his head. Yes, it hurt, but I didn't make a big deal of it. (I told you I was suffering for Jesus.) I made sure he was okay, and the game continued.

The camp ended, and I returned home. On one of my first evenings back, my wife and I were sitting on the couch when she looked at me and said, "You have a crack on your front tooth." I didn't believe her, so I took a look for myself. Sure enough, my left front tooth was cracked. When I went to the dentist, he told me the bad news: "It's not a question of *whether* your tooth will fall out, but *when* your tooth will fall out." He said I needed a crown put in (that's a fake tooth for all of you who don't know dental terminology), and it would require a "custom shading."

Several days later, I found myself in the basement of a strange-smelling, laboratory-like house in some subdivision. This is where the custom shading would take place. A woman examined my teeth, took notes, and compared colors so the new tooth would match the old one. Apparently, the shades of my teeth are so complicated that I needed the new tooth to be customized!

This reminded me of something. The color of my teeth isn't the only unique thing about me: I'm unique. I'm special. I'm unusual. I'm exceptional. And so are you. This isn't prideful thinking. Our loving God uniquely created each one of us. What's more, when we surrender our lives to God and seek to follow Jesus, he does something exceptional in us: He makes us into something new. We're "born again," as Jesus explained to Nicodemus (John 3).

> *Following Jesus is doing what he has asked of us and doing as he would do.*
>
> —Jodi, 15

If you've given your life to Christ, the King of kings has customized you. Your identity has changed. Like a caterpillar turned butterfly, you're beautifully made. You can fly in freedom. You're a new creation not sometime in the future, but *now* (2 Corinthians 5:17).

The Real You

Sometimes we trick ourselves into thinking we're not anything special. Sometimes we beat ourselves up with guilt and grief. Especially during your teenage years, you might look in the mirror and dislike what you see. When we're not living faithful lives for God, the Holy Spirit will convict us and point us back to the right path with Jesus. But at other times, we need to be reminded of who we are because of our relationship with Jesus, our position in Christ as a result of his grace. This free gift puts us in a special, customized place.

Years ago, I got the opportunity to walk the ruins of the biblical city of Ephesus in Turkey. We saw places where people had worshiped false gods, as well as a partially standing library with Greek inscriptions. I fantasized about taking home one of those huge blocks of marble with cool Greek letters, but it didn't happen.

The highlight of the trip was walking into the large theater where the city people would gather for dramas and city council meetings. The book of Acts tells us that when Paul was in Ephesus, his truthful words about Jesus caused a riot. Paul had to escape by boat to save his life (Acts 19:21—20:1). Later, Paul wrote a letter to the Ephesian Christians describing their real identity. That letter is what we now know as the book of Ephesians.

Paul's words to these believers can help us remember our true identity as well. It's almost as if there's a thread woven throughout the book that describes the real you in connection to Jesus. Let's look for it together.

At the beginning of the letter, Paul states that he is writing to the holy people of Ephesus (Ephesians 1:1). At first, this might seem strange. Maybe you've grown up in a tradition that uses the word *saints* to talk about holy people who've died. But Paul isn't writing to dead people; he's writing to people who are alive in Christ. Because of their relationship with Jesus,

> *Jesus is the ultimate example of love and a servant in action. Jesus loved us enough to spend thirty-three years on earth as a human, without the comforts of being solely divine, because he loves us.*
>
> —Jimmy, 23

their real identity is that of a saint. That's true for you too. God sees you as completely clean because Jesus died for your sins. *You are a saint.*

Paul points out that those who follow Jesus are blessed "with every spiritual blessing" (1:3). Do you feel blessed? He doesn't mean blessed with material possessions, but something greater. When you become a follower of Jesus, your insides change. Peace, comfort, and joy invade your heart. You move from darkness into light. These are spiritual blessings in Jesus. *You are blessed.*

Have you ever been chosen last? Maybe it was on the athletic field or in the classroom. Well, God reverses the order. The real you was chosen first. Paul tells us we were chosen "before the creation of the world" (1:4). No matter what your history, in God's heart you're chosen because you're extremely valuable. He loves you. *You are chosen first.*

One of my nieces is adopted. I still remember when my sister and brother-in-law went to pick up Abby. They had to make preparations, pay bills, and sign papers. Paul tells us God has "predestined us for adoption to sonship" (1:5). For God, adoption is final. You and I cannot be *un*adopted. God will not turn his back on you. You are his child. *You are adopted.*

And as Paul reminds us a few verses later, God's forgiveness comes along with this adoption (1:7). Pastor and author John Piper says forgiveness is like a hug. Whenever my wife and I get into a disagreement—or what we sometimes call "intense fellowship"—I know we've reconciled when we finally hug. It's only when she and I face each other and embrace that I know full forgiveness has taken effect. The moment we ask God to take away our sins through Jesus's death on the cross, we're free. *You are forgiven.*

Alive in the Spirit

Has anyone ever asked you to do something without giving you the stuff necessary to do it? Maybe your friend asked you to wash his car but didn't give you a hose, soap, sponge, and towel to accomplish the job (or quarters to use in the automatic car wash). Well, Paul assures us God doesn't do that. He tells the Ephesians—and us—that we've been given all we need to follow Jesus. Paul tells us we're "marked in him with a seal, the promised Holy Spirit" (1:13). God doesn't ask you to live without a counselor, leader, and friend to guide you along the path of life. *You have been tattooed with the Holy Spirit.*

And in that Spirit, Paul tells us we've been made "alive with Christ" (2:5). I don't understand why some who follow Jesus seem dead on their feet. One of the reasons Jesus died for us was so we could be alive. The real you isn't comatose but overflowing with the fruit of the Spirit (Galatians 5:22–23). *You are alive.*

I'm sure the Ephesian followers of Jesus must have been depressed sometimes. Like each of us, they must've occasionally felt down in the dumps and forgotten their identity. But Paul reminds them—and all who follow Jesus—that God has "raised us up with Christ" (2:6). The moment we chose to follow Jesus, we were lifted to a new playing field. We were once in the street, but now we're in the stronghold. Our heads were down, but now

> *Jesus is God and Jesus is God's Son. Jesus is loving and full of grace. Those who follow Jesus are attempting to follow the example he gave us while he was here and are living to worship him.*
>
> —Deb, 28

they're up. No matter what your outward circumstances, you've been raised from death to life just as Jesus was raised from the dead (Philippians 3). *You've been lifted up.*

Paul also tells the Ephesian followers of Christ that they've been given a special gift: grace. He says, "For it is by grace you have been saved, through faith—and this is not from yourselves, it is the gift of God" (2:8). Think about the gifts you receive on Christmas morning. When was the last time you received a gift you'd earned and deserved? I love Christmas because it's a time when grace is expressed—most of the gifts are given freely with nothing asked for in return. In the same manner, salvation is yours because of Jesus's grace. It was unearned and undeserved. You had nothing to do with it. *You are full of grace.*

God's Handiwork

In chapter 2, I told you a bit about my visit to the Louvre with some students. For hours, we took in the sculptures and pieces of antiquity, including a number of Grecian works from Paul's time. Perhaps we looked at some of the same artwork Paul had in mind when he wrote the church in Ephesus, saying, "We are God's handiwork" (Ephesians 2:10). Look in the mirror and tell yourself, *I was made by the hands of God.* It really is amazing to think that the God of the entire universe took the time to knit each one of us together before we were born. He cared enough to number the hairs on your head, design your nose, place your ears, dye your eyes, paint your face, position your lips, and even determine the exact shade of your teeth—and that's just your head. *You are a work of art.*

But you're not just a body; you're also a spiritual being who has "direct access" to God (2:18). How amazing is that? It's like God has given us a backstage pass. As a result of our relationship with Jesus, we now have something hanging around our hearts that gives us permission to go to God anytime we like. It's called the Spirit. Because you have the Holy Spirit living inside of you, the real you can communicate with the Creator of the universe. In fact, Paul goes on to say that "we may approach God with freedom and confidence" (3:12). That's something special. *You have access to God through prayer.*

Your Place in the World

I'm grateful to be a citizen of the United States. This residency is special, but it's nothing compared to Paul's words to the Christians in Ephesus about their place in the world. He says, "You are no longer foreigners and strangers, but fellow citizens with God's people and also members of his household" (Ephesians 2:19). You might sometimes feel like you're out of place in this world, but Paul says we're connected to a family of believers in Jesus called the church. *You are connected to community.*

Finally, toward the end of Paul's letter to the Ephesians, he reminds them that they've been made righteous and holy (4:24). The divine thread of the "real you" started back in the very first verse of the book with the words *holy people.* And in verse 4:24, he defines those words: "like God in true righteousness and holiness." Being made right before God by grace through faith in Jesus puts us in a place of holiness. In God's eyes, you're holy. Can you believe that? We are set apart for Jesus. As a result, you can be confident in your position in Jesus. *You are set apart.*

Your real identity is in Jesus. This makes you out of the ordinary. In another one of his letters, Paul reminds believers that the mystery of Jesus Christ was made known to them. Not only that, but the God of the universe, who came to earth in human form, lives inside of them—and inside of you (Colossians 1:27). This should give you great hope and excitement as you follow Jesus for the long haul. *This is the real you.*

> *Jesus is a saving God who is just and caring.*
> —Bradley, 17

QUESTIONS FOR THE JOURNEY

1. Think about a time when you were one of the last ones chosen for a team or task. How did it make you feel? How does it feel to know you've been chosen first by God?

2. What makes it so difficult for us to realize how special we are in God's sight? Why do you think it's so hard for us to be content with who God designed us to be?

3. Look back at the italicized phrases at the end of each paragraph. Which descriptions of the real you are the most challenging for you to accept? What could you do this week to "nail down" your identity in Jesus?

CHAPTER 5

Doubt: Those Uncertain Moments

Everyone doubts. No matter how strong your faith, sometimes you get that feeling that God just isn't real. If you don't struggle with that, then I doubt you're really chasing him. It's doubt that makes faith stronger, when you're lying in your bed wondering why you're praying—and you keep praying anyway because your faith is more than feelings.

—David, 18

Then the eleven disciples went to Galilee, to the mountain where Jesus had told them to go. When they saw him, they worshiped him; but some doubted.

—Matthew 28:16–17

A Disciple's Hesitation

It happened. It was done. Finished. Complete. Fulfilled. The proof had been on display with eyewitness accounts for more than forty days (Acts 1:3). *Forty days!* That's longer than a month. That's longer than Christmas break.

Jesus's closest friends had seen him repeatedly after the resurrection. They knew he'd been crucified, yet there he was again—

alive. Put yourself in their sandals for a minute or two. Can you imagine seeing him again? You might have hugged him, shared a meal with him, laughed with him, cried with him, and heard him retell stories of events you'd seen firsthand. "Remember that storm on the lake?" he would say. "Remember the faith of Peter?"

As he spoke, you couldn't stop staring at him. As he served you the bread on the beach (John 21:13), you couldn't take your eyes off the holes in his hands. He was walking among you again. There was no reason for you to doubt the tomb was empty and Jesus was alive.

> *I never have doubts about following him. My doubts usually lie to me and tell me I'm not doing this Christian walk right. I feel insecure, inadequate, as if I'm not equipped to serve the Lord, or I'm not smart enough. But usually when I get back to God I'm more secure and reassured; I'm just where he wants me.*
>
> —Annie, 29

But according to Matthew, some of those closest to Jesus *did* doubt. Listen to his account of one of the final commissioning speeches from Jesus to his disciples: "Then the eleven disciples went to Galilee, to the mountain where Jesus had told them to go. When they saw him, they worshiped him; but some doubted" (Matthew 28:16–17).

Remember, this wasn't the first time the disciples were with Jesus after he rose from the dead; they'd been with him before. One time it was with a crowd of more than five hundred people (1 Corinthians 15:6)! Yet Matthew tells us some doubted. *Some doubted?* Why? How? These men and women had been with Jesus off and on for more than forty days. Yet they still had this place deep inside that questioned, that wondered, *Could all of this be true? Is Jesus really alive and in front of me? Is Jesus really the Messiah?*

And what about Thomas? He's mainly known as a doubter—a bummer of a description to have written on his tombstone. But his first reaction to hearing the news that the other disciples had seen Jesus alive was, "No way! I've got to see it for myself." Nothing happened for a week. A *week!* Thomas might have lain awake thinking about it every night that week, his doubts growing deeper each dark minute.

Then, finally, Jesus appeared to the disciples again—and this time Thomas was there (John 20:24–29). Jesus set up a personal worship experience with him. I can imagine Jesus addressing Thomas, "Tom, come over here and touch the holes in my hands. Put your fingers in my side. Feel that? That's from the spikes and spear. What do you think, Tom?" John tells us that doubting Thomas responded, "My Lord and my God!"

I have doubts about God when "good people" do stupid things that have bad consequences and it kind of seems like God doesn't care. Then I read of similar problems in the Bible and, in the end, God always had a good solution.

—Jodi, 15

Do you think Thomas ever doubted again? We don't really know. Maybe he did. But on that day he understood the true identity of Jesus.

What to Do with Doubts

Doubts about spiritual things come in all shapes and sizes. There are big doubts that plague all of us and hang around for a while. There are smaller doubts that quickly come and go. I imagine that sometimes when you've prayed, you've felt as though the prayers just bounced off the ceiling. I know I've had that feeling. You might be questioning if you're heading to the right college or accepting the right job. Maybe you're wondering why that terrible tragedy happened or questioning whether God even cares about the details of your life.

Doubts make their way in. You can do your best to ignore them and get past them, but they keep knocking at the door of your heart. As a believer in Jesus, you might think, *I'm not supposed to doubt, right?* You might feel like others look to you for answers, but you're filled with questions of your own. You begin to beat yourself up with guilt. *What's wrong with me? Why do I doubt God? I'm a believer. What will my friends and family think of me?*

If you're struggling with doubt, I'd encourage you to relax. Take a deep breath. Doubts are a normal part of the journey with Jesus, and they're especially common in times of transition. As you head out the door, customizing your life into all that God would have it become, you'll face doubts. But your identity is in Christ, and placing your faith in him will help you work through those doubts.

Remember: Doubt is not the opposite of belief. The opposite of belief is *unbelief.* Authentic faith says, "I doubt like the rest, and I'll be honest with my feelings." I think the disciples were honest about their doubts, and Jesus helped them along as they kept following him. Maybe he had to hang around for forty days after the resurrection just so they'd be convinced he was alive! The key is to stay true to your deep belief in God and follow Jesus wholeheartedly, even when doubts creep in. Don't run away from God when you doubt; use those times as an opportunity to get closer to Jesus like Thomas did. Get close enough to touch his hands and side.

> *In the back of my mind it often still seems too good to be true. Or I doubt my adequacy or worthiness to be one of his sheep. Why did he choose me? In the past year I've learned Jesus will accept me for who I am. Why can't I do that? He accepts all of me. God is love. This is a very simple but profound revelation.*
>
> —Rob, 26

Deal With Doubt

Here are some tips to help you handle those times when you find yourself struggling with doubt.

Acknowledge the doubt. Don't deny it. Don't be embarrassed. It's normal to doubt. Think about the most mature Jesus-followers you know—the people you most admire and look up to because of how they love Jesus and people. There's a good chance those folks have experienced doubt at times. Share your questions with them and ask them to share how they've dealt with their own doubts. I hope they can admit some of their doubts to you. If they can't, then they're not being real with you. It's worse to pretend you don't doubt. Give yourself room to think through your questions and struggles.

Admit your doubts to God. Don't just lie awake at night worrying. Talk to him. Tell him your feelings. He's God. Just like any other relationship, your relationship with God will grow with communication. Tell him your doubts in your own words. You won't shock him—he already knows your thoughts and the feelings of your heart. So just go ahead and claim them. Ask him to walk with you through the dark valley of doubt.

> *Most of my doubting comes in at the most likely place: Could Jesus really be the Son of God? It's hard to for anyone to comprehend God himself coming to earth in human form. I deal with this through prayer, asking God to remove my doubtful thoughts.*
>
> —Jaclyn, 17

Go to good resources. Spend some time in Scripture with your questions. In the back of most study Bibles is a concordance that includes some key themes and Scripture verses on various topics. Do your questions line up with some of these topics? Look them up in the Bible. You'll probably find that many people of the Bible have already asked the questions that plague you.

Nail down the essentials of your belief in Jesus—the real certainties. You and I don't know everything there is to know about God—we know about a thimble's worth. You may never receive answers to all of your questions and doubts this side of heaven, and that's where faith in God comes into play. Authentic followers of Jesus live with the tension and mystery that is God—accepting that God is God and we're not. Continue striving to know God, but recognize there are some things you might not know this side of eternity. When you doubt, make a list of the essentials of your faith in Jesus. Hold on to this list for a rainy day. When doubts and doubters come along, remind yourself of the most important things.

Doubts will come and go. Admit you have them. Talk to God, talk to good friends, and understand the most important aspects of your faith in Jesus. Dwell on him. Fill your mind with true, noble, right, pure, lovely, admirable, excellent, and praiseworthy things (Philippians 4:8).

Remember, God really is in control—even when you don't understand what he's doing. That's why I'm so glad he's God and I'm not. I would've messed it all up a long time ago. God is the God of answers, but sometimes I think he thought up all the questions too—so ask away. There's no question he hasn't already dwelled on. He would love to journey with you and your doubts.

QUESTIONS FOR THE JOURNEY

1. Do you see doubting as good or bad? Do you think it's okay to doubt some things as a follower of Jesus?

2. Can you identify areas that are causing doubt in your life?

3. What are some ways you can bring peace to your doubts this week? How can God help you?

CHAPTER 6

God's Will: His Design for You and Your Future

We all need to stay connected to God and use the gifts he's given us.

—Ryan, 24

Do not conform to the pattern of this world, but be transformed by the renewing of your mind. Then you will be able to test and approve what God's will is — his good, pleasing and perfect will.

—Romans 12:2

It All Starts in Kindergarten

One day I went to visit my daughter's kindergarten classroom. It's such a joy to spend time closely watching a group of five-year-olds.

At one desk there was a little girl absorbed in finger painting. Her eyes were bright with excitement over the mix of colors and the feel of the paint on her hands.

Over in the corner, two boys were building a tower with blocks. One of them stacked the blocks rapidly, with little care for the finished product. The other boy went out of his way to straighten up the messy construction made by the first. They needed no supervision.

Out on the playground was the class prankster. He loved to take the ball away from the girls. He'd run around in victory like he'd captured a great treasure, obviously hoping to provoke a response; but his audience seemed more annoyed than anything.

> *God will show you his plan for your life. Keep your eyes open.*
>
> —Rachel, 15

Back in the classroom a child sat all by herself, looking at a book. It's not that she was shy, sad, or bored. She seemed to love spending time by herself and was content to be alone.

Now fast-forward to the future. Let's imagine we could meet up with all of these kids a few years after they've graduated from college. Let's assume they're all Christians who are seriously committed to following Jesus. They're customizing their lives according to God's will.

Remember the little finger-painting girl? As an adult, she works as a buyer of textiles for a clothing manufacturer. She loves to arrange colors and patterns.

The two boys who were building with blocks are headed into the corporate world. One is a salesman bent on exceeding performance goals. The other will always be a refiner, a straightening-things-up, maximizing-effectiveness sort of guy. He works as a project manager at a nonprofit organization.

> *God reveals his will when you spend time with him in prayer and in his Word. God will also speak to you through those around you, which makes it very important to find a community of believers and mentors who can speak truth into your life.*
>
> —John, 23

The class prankster? He's a youth pastor. His love of joking around and turning heads (and his desire to be the center of attention) is now used to reach people for Jesus.

Finally, there's the girl in the corner who loved solitude and silence. She's now a magazine editor who's just written her first book.

All of these kids took the skills and interests they had as children, honed and refined them over time, and use those gifts for God's glory today. They've all discovered the will of God for their lives, the way he designed each one, the way he wants each one to be.[1]

God's Will for You

What do you remember loving to do as a child? Did you like to play with friends? Go fishing? Write poems? Tell jokes? Build things? Use your imagination? Draw pictures? Win games? Make new friends? Read? Help Mom and Dad landscape the yard? Talk to squirrels?

The point of all this questioning is this: God placed certain interests inside of you. It was his idea. It wasn't a mistake. The psalmist declares to God:

> I praise you because I am fearfully and wonderfully made;
> your works are wonderful,
> I know that full well.
> My frame was not hidden from you
> when I was made in the secret place,
> when I was woven together in the depths of the earth.
> Your eyes saw my unformed body;
> all the days ordained for me were written in your book
> before one of them came to be.
>
> Psalm 139:14 – 16

The desires in the hearts of those kindergarteners are no accident. God formed each and every one of those children in his or her mother's womb. It's the same with you. He formed you and knows you. He has a specific plan for you, and he's been preparing you to fulfill this plan. You were created by God's hands for God's glory. After coming to know Jesus as the Lord of your life, you are set to do the good works he has planned for you. The awesome thing is those good works are often in line with your heart's desires —maybe

---

[1] This illustration was inspired by my own experiences with my children and the stories in Arthur F. Miller Jr.'s book *Why You Can't Be Anything You Want to Be* (Zondervan, 1999).

even the same desires you had back in kindergarten. That's how God designed you.

A Savory Buffet

You've probably wondered, *What am I going to do with the rest of my life? What's God's purpose for me?* These questions about God's will for your life are very important. But I think we sometimes feel paralyzed by them. We're afraid of missing out on God's plan for us. We're rolling along on the highway of life, and we're afraid the path to God's will for us is a single, tiny dirt road marked by a lonely weather-beaten sign. We're afraid we might miss our exit and never find our way to the purpose God has in mind for us!

It's very important to keep our eyes and hearts open for the signs that can point us toward God's hopes and dreams for us. We'll talk more about that later. But I don't believe God's will for each one of us is found along a single path that's easy to miss. I think God's will for us is more like a buffet at the nicest restaurant in town. Can you picture it? It's like a huge table stretching as far you can see, with every possible appetizer, entree, and dessert available. It doesn't get any better than this! It's *all* God's will, and he's saying, "Come eat. Start wherever you'd like and eat till your heart's content." Is this the way you picture the will of God for your life? Or do you see it more like a cheap fast-food meal with few options (with ketchup or without)?

I used to think God's will for me was very specific. I was supposed to be a teacher at a Christian school (I'm not), coach soccer (I don't), live in Michigan (no again), get married (I did!), have two children (add one more), adopt a dog (check), and live in a house with a white picket fence (a house, yes, but no fence). I thought if I were anything else, I'd be out of the will of God. Do you know what I mean?

> *Just stay open to the things he shows you. Eventually, it'll all come together, and then you'll know what you have to do.*
>
> —Shae, 18

Maybe you've felt the same way— maybe you've been living in fear of missing God's will instead of feeling the freedom to live in it. I've since changed my mind. The more I get to know the heart of the Father by studying the Scripture and daily experiencing his goodness, the more I'm convinced his will is a buffet. God is saying, "Eat till your stomach is satisfied, and then enjoy some more of me."

> *I pray and listen to God, looking for signs that line up with the situation.*
>
> —Brooke, 17

I hope I'm creating freedom in your heart. God knows the plans he has for you. For God that plan may be very specific (Ephesians 2:10), but for us it should seem like a buffet of options. We're simply to live in obedience to all he asks us to do based on Scripture and the Holy Spirit's direction. God has prepared a wonderful meal for you. So go get your buffet on!

Do you wonder where to start eating off the buffet? Perhaps whether you should start with the appetizer, main course, or dessert? Maybe you're afraid you're actually eating out of the dumpster behind the restaurant without realizing it. Below are some guidelines to calm your fears and give you confidence. Let's walk together through several scriptural principles that address God's will for your life. Pray and meditate on them as you read.

Direction

It all starts with our desire to do the will of God. The psalmist declared, "I desire to do your will, my God; your law is within my heart" (Psalm 40:8). We need to humbly open ourselves up to learning like the psalmist did when he wrote,

> Teach me to do your will,
> for you are my God;
> may your good Spirit
> lead me on level ground.

Psalm 143:10

We need to ask God to help us know where his buffet is located and where the boundaries between good food and spoiled food lie. This is a heart check for us: Are we passing up good food, maybe going through the motions of following God? Or do we really desire to do God's will, to eat from the buffet by following Jesus for the long haul?

With this desire to eat from God's buffet and an understanding that God will guide us to where the "good food" is located, we can now live in his will. Living in the center of God's will is about becoming holy, or "set apart" (1 Thessalonians 4:3–8). This means becoming more like Jesus and actively seeking to set yourself apart for God in your choices and relationships.

God wants us to identify with Jesus in every area of our lives. This will certainly involve bringing others to the buffet and serving them along the way. When we see a need, we're to jump in and serve. This is what loving God and loving others is all about (Mark 10:43; John 13:1–17). This is being in the center of God's will.

Getting Specific

Following Jesus for the long haul means taking God's words to heart. It means needing God like our bodies need air and water. The writer of Proverbs echoes this sentiment:

> My son, if you accept my words
> and store up my commands within you,
> turning your ear to wisdom
> and applying your heart to understanding —
> indeed, if you call out for insight
> and cry aloud for understanding,
> and if you look for it as for silver
> and search for it as for hidden treasure,
> then you will understand the fear of the LORD
> and find the knowledge of God.

Proverbs 2:1–5

Another Proverb that gives us insight into God's desire for us reads,

> Trust in the LORD with all your heart
> and lean not on your own understanding;
> in all your ways submit to him,
> and he will make your paths straight.

Proverbs 3:5–6

In other words, live your life for Jesus by obeying his teachings and living a life of service to him. Do this and he'll give you clear direction for your journey.

Sticking close to Jesus isn't always easy as you head into the unknown after high school. Difficulties are ahead of you. There may be times when you feel alone, but that's when you most need to lean on God's promises tucked away in Scripture.

In the book of Romans, Paul writes that we're to offer ourselves as "living sacrifices" (12:1). Even when it gets hot and uncomfortable, we need to die to ourselves and live for God. If we do this, we're worshiping. And in doing this, Paul promises that we'll know God's will for our lives:

> Therefore, I urge you, brothers and sisters, in view of God's mercy, to offer your bodies as a living sacrifice, holy and pleasing to God — this is your true and proper worship. Do not conform to the pattern of this world, but be transformed by the renewing of your mind. Then you will be able to test and approve what God's will is — his good, pleasing and perfect will.

Romans 12:1–2

God's Specific Will for You

Do you want to know God's will for your life? Stop and think about that question. Do you want to find your God-given sweet spot?

If the answer is yes, you're already eating from the buffet. As you grow closer to God and serve people for the long haul, God will reveal gifts, passions, talents, and dreams to you. As part of the body of Christ, God will give you opportunities to use the gifts you've been given for his purposes. Listen to Paul continue in that same chapter of Romans:

> For by the grace given me I say to every one of you: Do not think of yourself more highly than you ought, but rather think of yourself with sober judgment, in accordance with the faith God has distributed to each of you. For just as each of us has one body with many members, and these members do not all have the same function, so in Christ we, though many, form one body, and each member belongs to all the others. We have different gifts, according to the grace given to each of us. If your gift is prophesying, then prophesy in accordance with your faith; if it is serving, then serve; if it is teaching, then teach; if it is to encourage, then give encouragement; if it is giving, then give generously; if it is to lead, do it diligently; if it is to show mercy, do it cheerfully.
>
> Romans 12:3 – 8

Paul is telling you to stay humble and evaluate the gifts and abilities God has given you. This process takes time as you serve and try new areas of ministry. Ministry isn't just a job for full-time pastors and missionaries; God wants every follower of Jesus to discover and use his or her gifts for his glory.

The moment you surrendered your life to Jesus, you were given gifts to use to advance the kingdom. We all need to discover these gifts as we serve in the local church, campus ministry, and everyday life. These gifts are connected to passions, desires, dreams, natural abilities, and talents.

God's specific will for your life is already planned. Just relax and live for him. Continue to discover what it means to eat from the buffet by talking to him continually, reading the Scriptures consistently, and obeying always. How fulfilling is that? Doesn't this take a load off your shoulders? It's only after looking back on a portion of our lives that we see clearly how God was guiding us in his divine direction.

Rest in the fact that God has a specific future in mind for you that incorporates your passions, dreams, gifts, and natural talents for maximum kingdom impact. Surrender, serve, and pursue God with all you've got. God promises to do the rest.

QUESTIONS FOR THE JOURNEY

1. Growing up, what did you know about the will of God?
2. Did any of the verses we looked at in this chapter stick out to you, challenge you, or help you? Which ones? Why?
3. How are you seeking God's general will for your life?
4. How are you seeking God's specific will for your life?
5. Try making a list of your passions, dreams, gifts, and talents. How do they point to your God-given design?

CHAPTER 7

Prayer: Talking With God

I test everything against what I see in the Bible and in God's charac-
ter and through prayer.

—Ryan, 24

Dear Jesus, help me to spread your fragrance everywhere. Flood my
soul with your spirit and life. Penetrate and possess my whole being
so utterly that all my life may be only a radiance of yours. Shine
through me and be so in me that every person I come in contact
with may feel your Presence in my soul. Let them look up and see no
longer me but only Jesus.

—John Henry Newman

Prayer Is Important

God wants to hear from you. Some people find prayer difficult, so
they don't talk to God on a regular basis. They think they need to
say the "right" words or sound like a prayer professional. Maybe
you're one of those people. Or perhaps you don't really know how
to pray and you don't know what to expect when you pray. Don't
feel too bad. If all the followers of Jesus were honest, they would all

say they struggle with the mystery of prayer. Did you catch that? In many respects, prayer is a mystery.

Prayer is simply communicating with God; but listening, requesting, and worshiping God in prayer is not always simple. He is the God of the universe. He is not just another human being (and communicating with people is hard enough!). He is the Creator of the universe who sent his Son Jesus Christ and worked in the hearts of people to write down the Bible. But he is also personal and longs to have relationship with his created beings. So don't beat yourself up about prayer—it's something we can all grow in over time.

Jesus Expects Us to Pray

Don't think of prayer as an impersonal requirement where we need to say the right things, in the right way, with the right tone and inflection, in the right physical posture, and at the right location or at the right time. No. Prayer is to a Person. Realize that it is to the One with all the authority who loves you deeply. Jesus expects us to pray because he longs for an intimate relationship with us.

Read these excerpts from Jesus's words in the Bible about his expectations for you to talk to him.

> "And when you pray …" (Matthew 6:5)
> "But when you pray …" (Matthew 6:6)
> "And when you pray …" (Matthew 6:7)
> "This, then, is how you should pray …" (Matthew 6:9)
> "So I say to you: Ask … seek … and knock …" (Luke 11:9)
> "Then Jesus told his disciples … they should always pray …" (Luke 18:1)

Imagine Jesus showed up in front of you. You can see him. You can touch him. What if he said he wanted and expected you to pray to him more? Wouldn't you become more consistent in your prayer life? The verses above are not just for those who lived during Jesus's time or within a few generations of his time on earth. They are for you. He is asking you to speak to him like a friend.

Paul on Prayer

Everyone is devoted to something. Most of us are devoted to many things at the same time. When you make something a priority—when you're willing to sacrifice to see it, do it, or experience it—you know there is deep devotion. It might be a sport. It might be a video game. It might be a subject you love. It might be a girlfriend or boyfriend.

What are you devoted to? Think about it.

I will never forget when my wife and I were dating. I would drive long distances to see her when she was attending college out of state. I would stay up late to be with her. I would do anything to talk to her on the phone. I would rearrange my schedule to have quality and quantity time with the one I loved. When we care enough about something, we will go to extreme measures to make it happen.

God expects our devotion to go toward something in particular. Do you know what it is? God says through Paul, "Devote yourselves to prayer" (Colossians 4:2). Those other devotions might be okay, but this one should be top of the list. Being devoted to prayer might seem like an item on your to-do list, but there is more.

Not only does God want us to be devoted to him in prayer, he longs for us to have a relationship with him in prayer. Paul says, "Pray continually" (1 Thessalonians 5:17). Like a habitual cough that occurs with a rhythm throughout the day, God wants us to "touch base" with him, talk to him, request of him, worship him, and listen to him like we would in any good relationship. Prayer is evidence of unbroken fellowship with God. How often do you text your best friend throughout the day? How often do you check in with them? Your love for God in prayer should go way beyond your texting habits with a friend.

Prayer Priority

The great reformer Martin Luther said, "As it is the business of tailors to make clothes and cobblers to mend shoes, so it is the business of

Christians to pray." It dawned on me years ago that prayer is not to be done out of duty but out of love, because the King of the universe is inviting us into his throne room for some fellowship with him. Listen to these words from the writer of Hebrews: "Let us then approach God's throne of grace with confidence, so that we may receive mercy and find grace to help us in our time of need" (Hebrews 4:16). Prayer is an extraordinary opportunity to humbly take your needs to the One who saved your soul. Like a peasant entering the king's quarters, we are coming before the King of kings in communication. It is an awesome responsibility and privilege.

Doubting Prayer

Why do so many believers admit that they struggle to pray? Sometimes it's a lack of discipline. It is hard work to maintain relationships with those you love. Sometimes you take them for granted; and before you know it, they are distant and you don't know them at all. The same can be true with God. You need to work to have a relationship with God by knowing him through the Bible and talking to him in prayer.

Other times people don't pray because doubt sneaks into their hearts. Let's be honest: We sometimes doubt that anything will actually happen if we pray. I've wondered if my prayers just hit the ceiling and drop to the ground. Have you? If we felt certain that God was moving a few seconds after we prayed in faith, every follower of Jesus would have holes in their jeans from kneeling on the ground in prayer. God does promise to answer prayer, but it's not always visible, and it's not always the way we wanted him to answer or in the timing we desired.

Occasionally people don't feel close to God, so they stop communicating with him. Our emotions are unpredictable. One day we wake up with joy on our lips; the next, for whatever reason, we're in the dumps. This is why it's so important to allow the Bible to dictate our emotions and not let our emotions drive our lives. Feelings are fleeting, but God's Word (the Bible) is steady and unchanging. *God* is unchanging. When we pray, we need to remind ourselves that he is faithful and just. He is in control. He has your best interest in mind because he loves you.

At other times, people struggle to pray because they don't really see the need to pray. Things are going well. Why do I need God? Sometimes we wander into this mindset, but Jesus said, "Apart from me you can do nothing" (John 15:5). Wow! Sometimes our pride gets in the way, and we think we can handle the good times and bad times on our own. But the truth is we need him when life is good just as much as we need him when life gets hard. Our relationship with him is the most important thing, and it is hard to have a healthy friendship without continual communication.

How to Pray

If you are discouraged about your prayer life, want to learn how to pray better, feel weak in your prayer life, or just want to grow closer to God, here are some thoughts to hang on to.

We learn how to pray by praying. I am scared to death of foreign languages. I know that might seem like a strange fear, but I just don't get them. I tried Spanish and was frightened by the idea of being called on in class to say *hola*. With this in mind, you and I both know that to learn a foreign language, we must speak it. Practice is critical. If you want to learn how to communicate more effectively with your friend, you must speak with your friend. Prayer is the same way. In your own words, speak with God as though he is your friend. Write down your prayers. Pray out loud. The first step toward growing in prayer is to start praying.

It helps to read prayers in the Bible. You can learn a lot from looking at how those in the Bible prayed. Meditate on the Psalms and see how David prayed: "Listen to my words, LORD, consider my lament" (Psalm 5:1). Read the beginning of Paul's letters in the New Testament. How did he pray for the recipients? You could pray the same things for your friends and family. Pray something like Paul prayed, "continually ask God to fill you with the knowledge of his will through all the wisdom and understanding that the Spirit gives" (Colossians 1:9). Who wouldn't want that prayer heading up to heaven on their behalf?

Pray with others. The disciples learned to pray by listening to Jesus and praying with one another. They said, "Lord, teach us to pray" (Luke 11:1), and Jesus taught them how to pray. Get around those you know who are connected to Jesus and listen to them pray. Ask God for the same kind of relationship and pray with them to gain confidence. Remember, God doesn't care if your speech is nice and smooth. He cares that you are talking to him.

It helps to read about prayer from others. There are many wonderful books on prayer from men and women who know how to pray. George Müller's prayer life was one of faith. David Brainerd's biography records a life motivated by prayer. John Wesley, Hudson Taylor, William Carey, and so many others were connected in prayer with their heavenly Father. There are many historical mentors of the past who had intimate connections with God. We can learn from them.

More Thoughts on Prayer

Jesus told us to pray like he prayed. He said,

> Our Father in heaven,
> hallowed be your name,
> your kingdom come,
> your will be done,
> on earth as it is in heaven.

Matthew 6:9 – 10

This kind of prayer is powerful and effective if we absorb it into our hearts and lives. We should pray that heaven comes to earth as Jesus taught us. How can we apply it to our lives? As believers we discover what is on God's heart by talking to him and studying the Bible. We harvest the fruit of the spirit already inside of us, asking God to bring it to the surface so that others experience love, joy, peace, patience, kindness, goodness, faithfulness, gentleness, and self-control (Galatians 6:22 – 26). This is a little heaven on earth.

Do you want your communication with God to get results? Here are some final tips to grow in prayer.

Pray with conviction. Sometimes we have wimpy, selfish, and small prayers. *Hello?* We're building a relationship and communicating through prayer with the God of the universe. If you're praying prayers that you know are lined up with God's words in the Bible, then go for it. In other words, if you're praying the same way Paul did or Jesus did or David did, then you know you are inside the heart of God. Prayer is not superstition or a magic act or a special formula or a key to unlock a safe. If you are a believer in Jesus and have a relationship with him, he longs to answer your prayers. Dare to believe that what Jesus told us to do will bring about change in our world for God's glory.

Pray with the Bible in mind. As I mentioned, God always answers prayers that are in harmony with the prayers of the Bible. The more you study the Word of God and know his heart for your friends, family, roommate(s), professors, and the world, the more effective your prayer life is going to be. If you begin to pray God's Word like Paul prayed for the Colossians, you will be amazed by what happens. Paul prayed asking "God to fill them with the knowledge of his will through all spiritual wisdom and understanding." He continued by praying that their "lives would be worthy of the Lord and may please him in every way" (Colossians 1:9 – 14). Try using biblical verses to pray for those around you and watch what God does.

Be specific in your prayers. It's easy to be lazy in prayer. Don't just say, "Lord, bless this day." Say, "God, help my dad with his anger issue. Fill his mind with the confidence that you are in control and give him peace that surpasses all human understanding through your Holy Spirit." How will you know that God has answered your prayers unless you're specific? Trust God enough to stop generalizing and tell him what's really on your heart. Specific prayers get specific answers.

Expect God to answer your prayers. Sometimes we pray and we don't look for answers because we really don't think it matters much. When you pray, anticipate an answer with your eyes open. God cares and he wants to answer you. When you pray, pray as Jesus prayed.

Prayer is one of those areas you'll need when making the transition into the real world. It's important because your relationship with Jesus depends on it. Imagine not talking to someone you love for weeks or months at a stretch. That relationship wouldn't work very well. Don't go an hour without talking with the Savior of your soul. He longs for a loving relationship with you, and prayer is a part of it.

QUESTIONS FOR THE JOURNEY

1. What comes to mind when you think about prayer?
2. What's the most difficult thing about prayer for you? Be honest.
3. How can you improve your prayer life today? Where will you start?
4. If you knew that God longs for you to listen to him and make requests of him — while knowing that he listens to you — what would you ask for today? Why not pray it right now?

PART TWO

Choices — Do My Decisions Matter?

I do my best to follow Jesus and try hard to make the right choices all the time.

— Bradley, 16

As you move on from high school, you'll gain a greater amount of power and control over your life. You'll have more freedom to make your own decisions. You probably long for such freedom, but there's a cost that comes with it. With this new freedom comes increased responsibility for your decisions and actions. And as so many great action movies illustrate, power can be used for good or bad, for productivity or destruction.

You're in the middle of a shift in power, control, and responsibility. You'll increasingly make the big decisions in your life and probably have mixed feelings about this. On the one hand, you likely can't wait to be on your own and away from the boundaries of the people who raised you. On the other hand, the people and structures you've been depending on up to this point will no longer be present in the same way. This might make you nervous, at least a little while.

Take a look at what a couple of people said as they looked back on that time of transition to life after high school:

> I'm in the first months of my transition to college, and it's much less dramatic than I expected. The hardest part is establishing myself as a follower of Jesus all over again to these new people. I had a large amount of freedom in high school, at least my junior and senior years, because I'd earned my parents' trust. This made the transition a lot easier.
>
> —David, 18

> No matter how well you do in high school or how great your friends are, it's not easy going to college and suddenly having all of this freedom (which is terrific) and responsibility (which can be good too). In high school, it was easy for me to shine because I had this amazing support network of friends and adults. You really have to build a new network of support after high school, when you're suddenly separated from your childhood friends and family.
>
> —Deb, 28

In this section, we'll talk about what good choices look like. I'll set you up to cruise into the real world and not crash and burn into adulthood. It's up to you to make the right choices, take on more responsibility, and wisely handle the new power you'll have.

CHAPTER 8

Worldview: Owning Your Faith

First you need to obey him; don't do your own thing. Then pray and seek after God for the future.

— Stephanie, 18

That is the message we need to press home to our friends and to our impressionable kids. They need to know that everyone embraces one philosophy or another — a worldview that defines his or her conception of the world, of reality, and of human life. These beliefs are woven into [our culture] — often in such subtle ways that [we] miss. That is why it's so important [for us] to find the worldview message in [everything].

— Chuck Colson

Finding Pirates

Years ago, my young son got a book called 1001 *Pirate Things to Spot*. It tests your observation skills. Similar to a *Where's Waldo* book where you look for Waldo on every page, in this book you look for pirates, parrots, cannons, swords, skull and crossbones flags, anchors, boats, and treasure. I loved sitting with Levi and looking for the striped pirates. The longer you look at the picture, the easier it is to see them. Over time, you learn where to look and where not to look. Your eyes are focused to look for pirates.

The same is true of truth—especially biblical truth in the world. The longer you look at the real Father, Son, and Holy Spirit of the Bible and not a counterfeit, lookalike God, the easier it is to see him in the world. When your view of God is clear, you find your eyesight to be clearer for finding him in the attitudes and actions of people. Making this distinction between the real and fake God is called *discernment*. As you head into the real world, you'll need a view of the world that is thoroughly biblical, because this world can be full of hurt, destruction, greed, jealousy, and pride.

In this chapter I want to help you nail down your worldview— what you believe and why you believe it. Your worldview will form your identity, choices, and belonging; and clearly identifying your worldview before you go out into the world will help you keep the faith and continue to mature well. You'll discover a variety of world-views on the college campus and in the real world. Classrooms and cubicles will be full of counterfeits. Below, we'll try to sort out these belief systems.

View of the World

Everyone has a view of the world: children, teenagers, and adults. A worldview, according to the dictionary, is "the overall perspec-tive from which one sees and interprets the world" or "a collection of beliefs about life and the universe held by an individual or a group."[1] Whether or not you think about it, your worldview is heav-ily influenced by your culture. As you can imagine, this makes for some widely varying worldviews across the world. I will focus on the major ones you'll encounter outside of high school, in order to equip you with a proper way to see the world through the precepts of the biblical God.

---

[1] Definition taken from the Free Dictionary (*www.thefreedictionary.com/worldview*).

I probably don't need to tell you that you'll continue to face various views of the world in the classrooms, workplaces, malls, grocery stores, gas stations, and coffee shops you visit. Many of you reading this book may have already encountered them in your daily life. Keep in mind, you might not hear the formal titles as I present them, but these worldviews still exist. Just listen closely to the way professors, friends, coworkers, and others talk about the way they see the world and make decisions. As you train your ear to listen to what people really believe, you might be tempted to follow these false beliefs as you continue to form your identity in college and afterward. Be careful. Don't be fooled. Knowing how to identify these different perspectives will help you understand where they come from so you can compare those sources and mindsets with your own beliefs and the reasons behind them.

All Physical

If you're heading off to a secular university, I'm confident you will run across humanists (people who believe in human reason, ethics, and justice, but who reject anything supernatural or attributed to God[2]) who believe in naturalism.[3] In naturalism, the material universe is all that exists. It's easy to remember this definition because it's an all-natural world. Reality is "one-dimensional." There is no such thing as a soul or spirit in this understanding of the world. Everything can be explained on the basis of natural laws and science. Humanity, emotion, and reason are the random by-products of a biological process of evolution (remember Darwin?). Truth is understood through scientific proof. Only things that can be observed through the five senses are accepted as real or true, leaving morals and values completely up to the individual, based on individual preferences or socially useful behaviors.

---

[2] Definition from *www.encyclopedia.thefreedictionary.com/Humanism +(belief+system)*

[3] Information for all of these worldviews was adapted from *Christianity: The Faith That Makes Sense* by Dennis McCallum (Tyndale, 1992).

Atheism is a form of naturalism in which one does not believe there is a God. Agnosticism (believing any ultimate reality is unknowable) also falls under this category. Naturalists don't believe there is purpose or meaning in life outside of human experience. Only individuals can shape their own destinies, and they must do so without the benefit of any absolute right or wrong (this is existentialism).

There is no God out there to guide or direct people, according to this understanding. For many naturalists, science is their god; but as Christians, we must remember that God is the Creator of the universe and puts his glory on display for us to experience. In doing so, he reminds us that there is meaning outside ourselves — a plan that stretches across eternity. The naturalist will declare there is no overall purpose but to "live it up" while we're on planet Earth because "this is as good as it gets." And elements of that philosophy are attractive even to us. So be careful. It's tempting to let parts of this worldview creep into our Christian perspective, but we must remember that a Christian lives for something more than himself.

All Spiritual

On the other end of the worldview spectrum are pantheists. They believe that only the spiritual dimension exists and all else is illusion or, as they call it, *Maya*. It is somewhat like the Matrix movies where a "spiritual" dimension is what's real, and the natural boundaries of the visible world don't exist. Pantheists would say there is an increased and unhealthy emotional connection to the world. Spiritual reality or *Brahman* is eternal, impersonal, and unknowable. It is possible to say that everything is a part of God, or that God is in everything and everyone. Humans are one with reality. Thus man is spiritual, eternal, and impersonal, because all is spiritual. A human's belief that he or she is an individual is an illusion. Truth is an experience of unity with "the oneness" of the universe and is beyond all rational description. Rational thought as it's understood in the West cannot show us reality. As a result, sometimes speaking to a pantheist about their belief system is like nailing Jell-O to a wall. You can't do it because the real world is all unknowable spiritualism.

Furthermore, many pantheistic thinkers don't believe there is much distinction between good and evil because ultimate reality is impersonal. Instead, disunity with one another and the world is "unenlightened" behavior and thus failure.

Pantheism is more popular in other areas of the world, but you might run into those who ascribe to these beliefs in a world that's increased its interest in the spiritual "mystery" religions. Hinduism, Taoism, Buddhism, New Age movements, and "consciousness" are forms of pantheism, but they might mix with other worldviews.

As Christians, we know there are parts of God and the Bible that are mysterious because he is God—infinite and therefore beyond our finite understanding. But we can still know what we believe. Don't be fooled into thinking that Christianity is a "blind leap of faith." There is real historical and philosophical evidence for Christianity to connect physically and spiritually to the world. After all, we are physical beings with a soul that lasts forever. Christians believe there is both a physical and a spiritual part to this world, not just the spiritual.

> **Naturalism ◄► Pantheism**

God Exists

Most people believe there is a god of some sort. Theists believe in an infinite, personal, and loving God who created a finite-material world for his enjoyment and glory. For obvious reasons, theism is very different than naturalism or pantheism. It's sort of in the middle: Not all material and not all spiritual, reality is both material *and* spiritual. The physical universe as we know it had a beginning, and it will have an end. Humans (with body, soul, and spirit) are the unique creation of God, created "in the image of God" (Genesis 1:27). This means we are personal, eternal, and spiritual with emotions and intellect. Truth about God is known through "revelation from God himself. For Christians, the primary source of this knowledge is the Bible." And truth about the material world is gained through revelation, the five senses, and rational thought. Moral values are the objective expression of an absolute moral being.

Christianity, Islam, and Judaism are expressions of theism. In short, Judaism was the chosen precursor to Christianity. The Jews are God's chosen people, and the Old Testament is full of stories about the Jews being directed through history toward Jesus's coming to earth. Islam is very different. Even though Muslims believe in one God (called Allah), they have a very different view of this God than the description in the orthodox Bible of the Christian faith. With the rise of an Islamic worldview in the United States and around the world, be wise and discerning. It's not good enough to be a theist believing in one God. How a worldview describes this God is extraordinarily important.

The Trinity in the Bible

Christians believe there is one God in three Persons: Father, Son, and Holy Spirit.

1. In creation (Genesis 1:2, 26)
2. In God's presence (Psalm 139:7)
3. In calling us to serve (Isaiah 6:8)
4. In atonement (Hebrews 9:14)
5. In giving us new life (Romans 8:11)
6. In baptism (Matthew 3:16 – 17; 28:19)
7. In our access to God (Ephesians 2:18)
8. In our election by God (1 Peter 1:1 – 2)
9. In the ongoing direction of our lives (2 Thessalonians 3:5)
10. In benediction (blessing/guidance) (2 Corinthians 13:14)

Theism is found everywhere. I pray you connect with believers in the One True God of the Bible (Father, Son, and Holy Spirit) at school, at work, and even as you head off to the college campus. It's important for you to know the One True God of the Bible and not give into counterfeit gods. It's one thing to say you're a theist, but it's another thing for you to believe in the God of the Bible who sent his Son Jesus as a substitutionary atoning sacrifice for our sins (John 3:16).

> **Naturalism ← Theism → Pantheism**

Many Gods

There is another worldview, one with many gods. The belief that the world is populated by spirit beings who govern what's happening is called polytheism (*poly* means "many," and *theism* means "god"). Demons and gods are the real reason behind "natural" events. Material things are real, but they have spirits associated with them. Man is a creation of the gods (not God) like the rest of the creations on earth. Truth about the natural world is discovered through the *shaman* figure that has visions telling him what the gods and demons of a particular tribe or people are doing and how they feel. Moral values take the form of taboos, which are things that irritate or anger various spirits. These taboos are different from the idea of "right and wrong" because it is just as important to avoid irritating evil spirits as it is good ones. Thousands of religions and superstitions around the world are polytheistic.

It might seem incomprehensible that you'd run into friends, parents, adults, roommates, coaches, or professors who are polytheistic in the most overt sense, but you'll certainly encounter this belief system at least in part. The long-running movie series Star Wars depicts sort of a polytheistic battle between good and bad. Anyone (good and bad spirits) can use the Force for positive or negative influence. As a more grounded example, if Christians have fallen into an unbiblical view of the world, they may attribute more power to Satan and his demons than God allows them to have. The cosmic battle for good and evil can seem even-sided. But with a biblical worldview, God is the Creator and by far the most powerful force in the universe.

Descriptions of the world as being a pull between good and evil without a sovereign God over all of it often signal polytheism. Be careful of this one. Sometimes Christians let dangerous forms of polytheism slip into their worldview.

> **Naturalism ← Theism → Pantheism**
> **Polytheism**

All Up for Grabs

Here is a worldview you might be familiar with: postmodernism, or the idea that reality must be interpreted through our language and cultural "paradigm." Therefore, reality is "socially constructed." The people around us, our history, and our understandings drive our reality. Humans are just along for the ride in this world. They're a product of their social setting.

Closely related to this idea is the philosophy of relativism, the belief that truth is up for grabs and up to individuals or groups to decide. Truths are mental constructs that are meaningful to individuals within a particular cultural paradigm, thus "truth is in the eye of the beholder." Truths from one culture or thought group don't apply to other paradigms. There are no universal foundations on which to base truth because there are no absolutes (except the ones they invent for themselves!).

Values, too, are part of our social construct. "If you decide that murder is okay, then it's okay in your cultural context," says the postmodern relativist. The only universal values of this worldview are tolerance, freedom of expression, inclusion, and refusal to claim to have the answers. Thus, their only absolute is that there are no absolutes. *Read that sentence again.* Do you get it?

As a reaction to "modern thought," which was more scientific and rational in nature, postmodernists tend to lean more on experience and feelings than on rational thinking. Although dangerous, this idea is appealing to a broad spectrum of people. Everyone reading this book will discover friends, professors, and other adults in their lives who believe in some form of postmodernism. Postmodern relativism can overlap with many of the other views of the world, and it's even woven its way into the Christian church today.

Some of the values of this worldview are tolerance, freedom of expression, and full inclusion. On the surface, these values might be attractive, but they can lead us toward beliefs and values that go against the teaching of the Bible. For example, many postmodern relativistic thinkers believe that everyone will be in heaven with God after they die. This is called universalism. However, the Scriptures clearly teach that belief in Jesus is the only way for someone to have eternal life, and that not everyone will be in heaven with God (John 14:6; John 3:16; Matthew 7:21–23; Acts 2:36–39).

Other postmodernists, reacting to foundational truths of the Christian faith, believe that certain absolutes of the Bible need to change to fit the culture we live in today. This tragic thinking is even creeping into local churches where some don't like the words *foundation* or *absolute* or *doctrine* to describe essentials of the faith. This is dangerous and can lead to wrong interpretations of the Bible. As you move into college and then out into the larger world, you will need clear discernment and wisdom. Use proper interpretation principles as you explore the applications of Bible study today so postmodernism doesn't creep into your worldview tomorrow.

I've seen a bumper sticker around my city that reads CoEXIST with symbols from all the major belief systems and religions from around the world forming the letters. "Let's just all get along in peace. Stop fighting. Tolerate one another. No one is wrong, so stop judging." These are the messages in front of you. This is a great picture of the relativism you'll experience in the classroom, and it will challenge your faith foundation in Jesus Christ. Though their proponents may coexist on this earth, opposing worldviews cannot coexist in truth. The idea that no one is right and every man must find his own path to God is the ultimate picture of false teaching that you will face in the world. The One True God revealed himself to us through his creation and the Word of God (Romans 1–2). It's important for you to nail down what you believe and hold on to your relationship with Jesus according to the Bible—not the feelings, theories, or opinions of intelligent professors or coworkers.

Postmodernism
↓
Naturalism ← **Theism** → **Pantheism**
Polytheism

Who Are You Following?

Another key idea regarding worldview is authority. Theism is the only worldview under which there is *One* authority outside of space and time and to whom all creatures are answerable. The naturalist says science or scientists are the authority (thus themselves), while pantheists say they answer to their individual "light" (thus themselves). Those who believe in polytheism don't have one God but many, and the god with the most authority is up for grabs (and that level of authority is up to them). And postmodernism, especially, attacks the idea of an ultimate divine authority because "postmodern thinking" essentially says you are your own god because you make the rules for yourself (again, the decision rests with themselves).

We as Christians believe the God of the Bible is the real, true authority who is outside of the limitations of a purely material world (not us). He is omnipotent (all-powerful), omnipresent (everywhere at the same time), and omniscient (all-knowing). As a result, he has the final authority and is absolute. This includes authority over human beings. He will come to judge the hearts of humankind one day, but he wants to be our Lord today. The Bible teaches that God is the ultimate authority of the universe and the teachings given to us in the Bible are his precepts and should be followed. Simple, right?

The difficulty arises because we, as fallen and sinful humans, inherently have trouble with authority. This is what got Adam and Eve into trouble in the first place (Genesis 3), and it's an important concept for you to understand and embrace as you interact with people in class, at work, or even at a coffee shop.

The truth is all of us have this tendency inside of us to dislike authority. Sometimes this takes the shape of an internal "developmental fight" to become an individual. This is natural, but you need guardrails of biblical truth so you don't fall off the mountaintop as you drive down the highway of life. Just like my computer defaults to 12-point Times New Roman font every time I start typing a Word document, we all tend to default toward the sin of a worldview that centers around ourselves: "I want total freedom to come and go whenever I feel like it because I am in charge." *Notice the number of times I showed up in the last sentence.* But I'm grateful that God loves me (and you!) so much that he didn't leave me guessing but provided all I needed for life and godliness through his Word that became flesh (John 1:1–4). His name is Jesus, and he should be your pure worldview heading into the real world (Colossians 1–2).

QUESTIONS FOR THE JOURNEY

1. What is your worldview? What do you believe about God?
2. Why is it important that you think deeply about what you believe?
3. Where do you anticipate your faith in Jesus being questioned or even attacked?
4. How can you be sure your faith won't blow away and you'll be able to defend the gospel with love and courage?

CHAPTER 9

Responsibility: Getting Wisdom

Surrounding myself with positive people who love Christ makes it easier to live my life better. I hate disappointing my parents, friends, and family, so thinking about things and their consequences helps me make the right choices. I pray that God will help me make those right choices in my whole life and that he'll be with me each step I take.

—Candice, 17

My heart says of you, "Seek his face!"
Your face, Lord, I will seek.

—Psalm 27:8

So Many Choices

Every human being has something in common: We all have the power of choice. We all get to determine the direction of our own lives.

My chocolate lab, Mocha, doesn't have that same capacity to choose. Yes, she can decide when she wants to eat or sleep, but she will never carry the same level of responsibility we do. She just lies around all day, mostly on our couch. Once in a while, she'll open an eye, eat some dog food, or take a walk, but she mostly sleeps. There are moments when I think being Mocha would be great. But in the end, I think having the free will to make choices is one of the greatest gifts God gives us.

> *I try my best not to be selfish and not ask others "What can you do for me?" but "What can I do for you?"*
>
> —Ryan, 24

As you leave high school, the options are endless. This is such an exciting time! The will of God is laid out in front of you like a Sunday buffet ready to be devoured. So why is there so much stress?

The stress likely comes from a number of sources, but it mostly stems from the importance and sheer number of choices to be made. With choices comes the "R" word. You know it. Go ahead and say it out loud: *Responsibility*. Some choices will happen quickly, some have already happened, and others won't come until you get down the road a bit. But the big choices you're making, and the responsibility that goes with them, are multiplying.

Everything boils down to choices. Some people choose to smoke, drink, party, ski, chat online, snowboard, email, vacation, text their friends, do drugs, or have sex now and think about the consequences later. These are all choices, some bigger than others. Yet in the end, your life is the sum total of the choices you made.

God created you to live a full and healthy life. He wants to help you make wise choices. Paul wrote to the church in Ephesus, "Be very careful, then, how you live—not as unwise but as wise, making the most of every opportunity, because the days are evil" (Ephesians 5:15–16). God wants to give us more and more wisdom so we can live the full life that Jesus came to offer to each and every one of us (John 10:10).

Little Leads to Big

Wise little decisions lead to wise big decisions. *Read that again.* As you make the leap from high school to the life that awaits you after graduation, you'll face all kinds of choices daily. If you're going to college, you'll decide how your dorm room is arranged, how you schedule your days, when you study, when you sleep, what habits you'll establish, whom you go out with on the weekends, how often you call home, how many meals to eat a day, how often to do laundry ... you get the point.

> *It's important to have good friends who keep me accountable for my choices.*
>
> —Jodi, 15

Some of these choices might not seem like a big deal, but let's think about laundry for a minute. If you decide to wait to do laundry until all your socks are stinky, you may be forced to wear flip-flops to class. You might think, *What's wrong with that? I love flip-flops!* Well, there's nothing wrong with them as long as you're not in the middle of a snowstorm. But unless you have fur on your toes, you'll probably want socks when you're walking in snow. I think you see where I'm going. If you make a dumb little decision, like waiting till the last possible second to do your laundry, you may pay for it later.

If you make wise decisions about the little things in your life, you'll have a much easier time making wise decisions when the big things come along. Laundry might be a small choice, but paying off your credit card every month, deciding to get married, or buying a home or a car are bigger choices you'll need to take responsibility for later. Develop the habit of being faithful in the little things. This will grow your wisdom for the bigger decisions later.

Making Smart Choices

As you grow in responsibility, here are some tips about making wise choices as you follow Jesus.

Remember, God is the source of true wisdom, and the Bible is his big story—his grand narrative. Start by reading the stories of Scripture and asking yourself, *What does this teach me about God and his wisdom? How can I apply this wisdom to my everyday life?* The book of Proverbs is full of wisdom to help you make the right choices. Try reading a chapter a day for the next month—there are thirty-one chapters in all.

Before you make a big decision, seek the advice of a few Jesus-following adult friends or mentors. (See chapter 19 on mentoring.) Be honest and open with them. Share your thoughts and feelings about the choice to be made. Allow them to pray with you and for you over a period of time before making the choice. Listen to their advice and take it to heart.

Take a look in the mirror. As you grow into a mature, Jesus-following adult, one who manages their time wisely and takes responsibility for their life, you'll need to be honest with yourself. Growing in maturity entails taking a careful look at the real you and the choices you're making. You might be able to trick yourself more easily than you can trick others. Be authentic. Be real. As you consider any decision, honestly ask yourself: *Will the choice I'm about to make help me love Jesus and love others better?*

> *I set goals for myself and then reach those goals.*
> —Jodi, 15

Take a look at God. We all need to pray about the choices we face. God knows you best and has your best interests in mind. He loves you, and you need to hide this truth deep in your identity. God is the King who has authority over your life, but he's also a Dad who's tender and compassionate toward his children. He's the King Daddy. You may need to pray about some choices for a few days or a few weeks; some choices may even require months or years of prayer. This might seem like forever, but the older you get, the faster time flies.

Stay patient. Listen for God's voice as you pray. Only a few people have heard God's audible voice; you might hear his voice as a still, small impression of peace in your heart. Jesus says his sheep know his voice because they've spent time with the Good Shepherd (John 10:1 – 18). Turn up your spiritual hearing aid. Pull out those spiritual Q-tips. Await God's response.

The Ultimate Example of Responsibility

Jesus spent his time doing things that really mattered. He lived his life moment by moment as a model for us. Needless to say,

Jesus was responsible and made wise decisions. He touched people. He healed people. He talked to people others shunned. He laughed with outcasts. He cried with sinners. He made time for people. He loved to hang out with his friends and celebrate too. After long days with the crowds and his disciples, Jesus would often get up early the next morning to pray for the day ahead (Mark 1:35). Did you know Jesus led a seminar on time management? Okay, maybe not a real twenty-first–century seminar, but he used teachable moments to show his disciples how to best use their time.

> *I surround myself with people who'll keep me focused and not attempt to lead me astray.*
>
> — Shae, 18

Do you remember the story of Mary and Martha? Jesus and the disciples came to the sisters' home. Upon walking through the door, Jesus noticed Martha frantically running from task to task like a chicken with its head cut off. Mary chose to spend her time at the feet of Jesus, listening to stories and fellowshipping with the disciples. When Martha started to complain that Mary wasn't working, Jesus told her, "Martha, Martha ... you are worried and upset about many things, but few things are needed—or indeed only one. Mary has chosen what is better, and it will not be taken away from her" (Luke 10:41–42).

According to Jesus, Mary got it right. Time is better spent with Jesus than focusing on temporal things. That's not license for you to tell your friend, "No, I can't help you clean the church because I'm reading my Bible." But it does mean you need to take Jesus with you *all day* so you can live every moment for him. Paul declares, "Make the most of every opportunity. Let your conversation be always full of grace, seasoned with salt" (Colossians 4:5–6).

The Wisest Choice

Many people ask the wrong question when it comes to making the smart choices. They ask, "Is anything wrong with this choice?" The better question is, "Is this the wisest thing for me to do?" If we want to be mature followers of Jesus, we need to take our focus off what's wrong and put our focus on God. To consistently make wise choices, you'll need to have a growing relationship with God.

The way to discern the wisest thing to do is to spend time with the Wisest One. Make a commitment now to spend time with God every day for the long haul.

I've heard it said that the person who kills time injures eternity. In other words, time wasted with poor choices has a negative impact on God's kingdom. As you grow into a spiritually mature adult, use your time wisely.

Take time to stop and think; it's a source of power.

Take time to play; it's the secret to staying young.

Take time to read the Word; it's the fountain of wisdom.

Take time to pray; it has the potential to change your life with God.

Take time to love and be loved; it's the way God designed you.

Take time to be friendly to everyone; it's the road to happiness.

Take time to laugh out loud; it's music to your soul.

Take time to give of yourself; life is too short to be selfish.

Take time to work hard; it's your response to all that God has given to you.

Take time and responsibility seriously as you leave high school and begin following Jesus for the long haul.

QUESTIONS FOR THE JOURNEY

1. How do you discern which choices are wise?
2. Where does wisdom come from? How does God's perspective on wisdom differ from the world's?
3. Is it easier for you to ask, "Is there anything wrong with this?" or "Is this a wise thing for me to do?" What's the difference?
4. How important are friends in helping you make smart decisions?

CHAPTER 10

Morality: Smart Behavior

The Bible is full of references to morality and immorality, purity and impurity. No, it might not address every specific issue on morality, but you can definitely get God's overall view of what his standard looks like from reading his Word.

—Adam, 23

Commit your way to the LORD;
trust in him and he will do this:
He will make your righteous reward shine like the dawn,
your vindication like the noonday sun.

—Psalm 37:5 – 6

Mind Your Ps and Qs

What is morality, anyway? The dictionary defines *morality* as "a set of standards of conduct that are accepted as right or proper."[1] But what about Christian morality? Is that any different? Should those who follow Jesus have different standards of morality than those who don't know Jesus as their Lord?

---

[1] Definition taken from *www.encyclopedia.thefreedictionary.com/Morality*

Each culture and society has its own set of written and unwritten rules, its own opinions as to what's right or authoritative. For example, most modern cultures would agree that murder is unacceptable behavior. But people might disagree about whether or not it's okay to steal from a grocery store if you need food, take revenge on a mean neighbor, or drink alcohol. Even within the body of Christ, we don't all agree on all issues of morality.

> *When in doubt, I look to Scripture, but most of the time I know when things are right and wrong. I don't mind waiting a decade for the right guy, and I don't mind telling all the wrong ones no. That's how I've always been, and I hope that resilience stays the same as I go on to college.*
>
> — Shae, 18

Take a look back at your high school years. I bet your friends had a set of unwritten rules to live by. They had certain understandings about whether it was acceptable or unacceptable to drink, smoke, have sex, go to parties, or listen to certain types of music. Even if you're a follower of Jesus, there's a good chance you had friends with different opinions on some of these issues. Maybe you chose to become friends with certain people (and avoided others) based on the moral choices they made. Am I right?

If you're a follower of Jesus, your moral standards should be rooted in him. Christian morality is centered on Jesus Christ and Scripture. Thus, the standard for our conduct isn't based on popular opinion, but on the life of Jesus. Our choices should line up with what Jesus thinks.

Jesus came to earth to bring life, not death. He came to bring a life that is full, healthy, exciting, and joyful. It's called "overflowing" or "abundant" life or "life to the full" (John 10:10). So the big question you need to ask yourself as you head toward adulthood is, *Are my choices guiding me toward an overflowing life as Jesus described it?*

Thinking Like Jesus

If we want our moral compass centered on Jesus, we need to change our way of thinking. Paul told the church at Philippi, "In your relationships with one another, have the same mindset as Christ Jesus" (Philippians 2:5). In other words, we need to do our best to think like Jesus.

If we can figure out what Jesus would say about a given situation before we act or speak, we're in great shape. Let's put this to the test. What would Jesus think about—

Deciding to make out with someone you just met

Telling a "little white lie" to protect a friend

Having friends over for a wild party when your parents (or later, roommates) are away

Stealing the final exam for a class you're taking, throwing it out the classroom window, and then picking it up after school so you ace the exam (A high school friend of mine actually did this!)

These are all real-life situations you or a friend might face. I know they're focused on the "negative" side of Christian morality, but it's important to decide ahead of time what we'd do based on what Jesus would think. But these questions don't apply only to the "don'ts." We might also ask these questions:

What would Jesus think about—

Staying after school to help your shop teacher clean up and store the equipment

Giving money to help a classmate who can't afford to buy lunch

Taking a short-term mission trip to help build houses in a poor community

A couple making a commitment not to have sex before marriage

I think Jesus would be pleased if you acted positively in these scenarios. This is where the rubber meets the road after you graduate and become a mature, Christ-following adult.

The Bible directly addresses a lot of the moral issues we face today, but some questions it doesn't. Still, I believe trying to think like Jesus really helps us — even with those issues the Bible doesn't directly address. I believe our pursuing the Jesus of the Bible makes all the difference in how we look at the world. This pursuit isn't just a one-time event, but a daily commitment. As you do this, your thinking will become more like the mind of Christ, and the lines of morality will become clearer.

> *A good way for me to stick to being morally pure is to ask myself (no matter how cliché it may be) "If Jesus were standing right there, what would he think?" or "Would I be embarrassed if Jesus saw me doing this?"*
>
> — Jaclyn, 17

Paul reminds us that Jesus is "the image of the invisible God, the firstborn over all creation. For in him all things were created" (Colossians 1:15–16). Through Jesus, God came to earth in human form. And through Jesus's death on the cross, we've been reconciled with God (1:20).

Have you ever wished you could see God? Maybe you think, *If he'd just appear in my bedroom one time, it would make a difference.* Well, God has appeared in our world, and his name is Jesus. Why did he? To bring people to himself; for his glory, honor, and delight. The cross brings life. The cross brings the lines of morality to our everyday lives through the guidance of the Spirit, who lives inside every follower of Jesus.

Defining Your Morals and Values

God doesn't leave us hanging; he guides us in our morality. The whole of Scripture directs us toward a moral, Spirit-filled, overflowing life (John 10:10; Galatians 6).

In Matthew 5–7, we find Jesus's greatest sermon, the Sermon on the Mount. These few chapters at the beginning of Matthew's gospel are the high standard that provides marching orders for those who want to be disciples of Jesus. In this sermon, Jesus focuses on the importance of not just our actions, but also the motives of the heart that lead to action.

At the very beginning of this famous sermon are a series of statements called the Beatitudes (Matthew 5:2–12). Jesus tells the gathered crowd that God's blessing is on those who are humble (the poor in spirit), tender (those who mourn), broken (the meek), godly (those who hunger and thirst for righteousness), forgiving (the merciful), clean (the pure in heart), and reconciling (the peacemakers). This isn't an easy list to live, and Jesus closes it by acknowledging that people may insult or persecute those

> *I have to ask myself, "Why I am doing what I'm doing?" Am I selfishly pursuing my own pleasures at any expense, or am I honestly doing things to love others? When what I'm doing turns into selfish obsession to get my own pleasures, morality has gone out the window.*
>
> —Ryan, 24

who live by these words. But he promises that those who base their actions in these characteristics will be blessed. These are incredible statements from the One who lived them out all the way to the cross.

I suggest reading the rest of the Sermon on the Mount. It will guide your lines of morality as you transition to maturity.

A Few Specifics: Honesty and Integrity

Let me get more specific for a minute. How important do you think honesty is? Is lying acceptable? Do your friends tend to lie? Are "little white lies" okay? Dishonesty has become the norm these days. How one determines whether or not it's okay to lie is based on individual circumstances, like protecting yourself or a friend. Instead of asking the question, *What would Jesus think of me lying?* we lie almost instinctively.

I've heard some young people say, "Everybody lies, and everybody knows that everybody lies." There's research to support that many teenagers and twentysomethings lie on a regular basis.[2]

---

[2] Dr. Chap Clark of Fuller Theological Seminary has done hands-on research in this area among adolescents, and it's documented in his book *Hurt: Inside the World of Today's Teenagers* (Baker, 2004).

But when those same people are asked if they're honest, they answer, "Yes, I'm basically an honest person." Yet their actions often tell a different story.

As you head into adulthood, you'll be tempted to lie in small and big ways. Maybe you'll be asked about your past work experience in a job interview, and you'll wonder

> *Morality is a BIG deal in my life. I think our culture looks at morality as a joke, but I take it very seriously. I see the consequences of making bad decisions.*
>
> —Candice, 17

if you should exaggerate in hopes of getting the job you've always wanted. Maybe you'll be tempted to tell your parents that your college grades are better than they really are. Maybe when your boss asks you a question at work, you'll lie without even thinking about it and lose your job. Perhaps the consequences will never be so quick and direct, but I assure you there *will* be consequences. In your pursuit of holiness, before lying ask yourself, *What would Jesus think of my lying in this moment?*

A couple of other temptation areas you'll wrestle with are integrity and trustworthiness. Have you or a friend ever cheated on a test? Maybe you gave an answer to a friend during a final exam. Or maybe it was something that seems even more trivial, like fibbing in gym class about the number of pushups you did. (According to national research, the rate of cheating among high school and college students is rising, though college students tend to cheat less than high school students do, according to some surveys.[3])

Draw the line now. As you become an adult follower of Jesus, choose not to cheat in any form. Minor cheating now could morph into cheating on your taxes in the future. That's how sin works—you think you're in control of yourself, but sin's really in control of you. This is why Paul told the followers of Jesus at Colossae, "Do not lie to each other, since you have taken off your old self with its practices and have put on the new self, which is being renewed in knowledge in the image of its Creator" (Colossians 3:9–10).

---

[3] Clark, Hurt, 152–156.

As a follower of Jesus, ask for God's help in making moral choices rooted in honesty and integrity. Make the decision now to avoid lying or cheating in any form, as that would prevent you from making a smooth transition into becoming an adult who whole-heartedly loves Jesus.

QUESTIONS FOR THE JOURNEY

1. Brainstorm a list of the immoral actions you see in the world. How does this list make you feel?

2. How do you determine your lines of morality? What's your measuring stick?

3. Do you know friends who've lied or cheated in the last few months? How do you respond to this behavior? What can you do to avoid falling into this trap?

4. What steps can you take to cultivate honest, encouraging relationships as you make the transition into the real world?

CHAPTER 11

Your Major: Figuring Out the Right Direction

It's okay not to know what you want to do right away! Value the advice and thoughts of your parents and friends, be flexible, and focus on God.

— Rob, 26

Trust in the Lord with all your heart
and lean not on your own understanding;
in all your ways submit to him,
and he will make your paths straight.

— Proverbs 3:5 – 6

The Black Hole

Every time my family goes to Sam's Club to shop, the kids ask my wife for a coin. (They know I never have any money.) I know where they're headed. There's this game where you drop a nickel in the slot and then get dizzy watching it go around. First, the coin makes long, wide circles at the top. I watch their eyes spin, and I get lightheaded.

Then the coin rolls around and around the bowl, each rotation becoming a little smaller. Finally, the coin spirals down through an open hole in the bottom.

So how do you choose your direction? If you're a college student, how do you select your academic specialty—better known as the dreaded major—knowing that it will shape your future career possibilities? This process looks a little like the coin game: You might think yourself in circles before you finally hone in on your center. As you wholeheartedly obey God and proactively look for his specific purpose for your life, as you explore different areas and interests and stay sensitive to God's leading, he'll draw you toward the center of his will for you. In the beginning you may feel like you're taking very long and broad rotations around your major, like an airplane circling an airport, stuck in a holding pattern as it prepares to land. That's the way it works. But over time as you move toward the center and as you gravitate toward subjects and classes you enjoy, you'll find your direction.

> *I had a major, went with it for a semester, and dropped it. Don't think you have to have your life all planned out when you're handed your high school diploma or GED. Many students change their major or transfer to a different school before they complete college.*
>
> —Gloria, 18

> *My first shot at a major was a combination of strengths that I'd seen evident in my life in high school: leadership, math, organization, and service. It all went together for business.*
>
> —Deb, 28

Areas of Discovery

Whether you're in high school or the early years of college, you already have interests that relate to your major-to-be. From the moment you were born, throughout elementary school, and all the way through high school, God has been molding you into who you are. If you've surrendered your life to Jesus and you're actively following him today, the Holy Spirit lives in you and guides you to your purpose.

Choosing a major can be an important part of determining your future career path. Here are some things to help guide you as you circle, searching for your sweet spot in the center of God's will.

First, look to *Scripture*. God will use your growing relationship with Jesus and your study of Scripture to help you grow into the person he wants you to be. For example, as you read the letter to the Galatians, you discover there are acts that lead to a sinful life and acts that lead to a fruitful life. Paul says the fruit of the Spirit is "love, joy, peace, forbearance, kindness, goodness, faithfulness, gentleness and self-control" (Galatians 5:22–23). After reading through this passage, you might find yourself confessing situations in which you've given in to sinful behavior, and then asking God to help you live a fruitful life. Something supernatural happens in this experience of study. God begins changing your character and, in doing so, reveals to you who you are and what you're supposed to do.

Second, look for *open doors*. These are the opportunities and experiences that are right in front of you. In college there are so many classes to choose from. You aren't expected to know what you're going to do with the rest of your life that first day you bust out of your high school's double doors. Your early college years are full of discovery. There are many general education classes you'll need to take to graduate, but you'll also have opportunities to take elective classes that let you explore different areas. The larger the university, the more classes you'll have to choose from.

In addition, look for opportunities to serve on or off campus. Getting paid is a bonus, but don't expect to make money during the discovery process.

Obviously, you want to try and figure out what God wants you to do. If that isn't clear when you enter college, pick something you enjoy. Most people change their majors a couple times throughout their college career, so it's not the end of the world if you want to change it after your first semester. However, be aware that some programs are a lot more rigid than others (nursing, education, etc.), and you could add significant time and money if you change too often.

—Adam, 23

Keep your eyes and ears open for God's divine appointments. He wants to help you find the college major and career direction that will best fit you and give you the greatest joy. Ask yourself, *What does the world need that's also a good fit with my abilities and interests?* This question might direct you toward an area of study and a major.

Third, look to your *heart*. As you take classes, stay in tune with the Holy Spirit's guidance. Keep asking yourself questions: *Do I enjoy this class? What do I like and dislike? Can I see myself working in this field for the rest of my life? If I could do anything I wanted for the rest of my life, what would it be?* Ask God to give you peace about your decisions.

The path your heart reveals may surprise you. When I was growing up, I didn't like to read. My mom tried everything to change that, but I always preferred being outside with a ball and playing sports like soccer, basketball, and tennis. In time, I began to enjoy reading as I found my areas of interest: theology and culture. You may find yourself drawn to something you didn't like at an earlier age.

Fourth, look to your *design*. Paul says that each of us is "God's handiwork, created in Christ Jesus to do good works, which God prepared in advance for us to do" (Ephesians 2:10). God has designed you to make a unique contribution in this world. With a consistent and growing relationship with Jesus, this design can be discovered.

As you step off the Tube trains in the United Kingdom, you will hear a recorded voice reminding riders to "mind the gap" when stepping from the train to the platform. Well, you also need to stay alert and "mind the GAP"—your Gifts, Abilities, and Passions. God has designed each one of us with spiritual gifts, natural abilities, and passions that are ready to be discovered and used in his service. It's our responsibility to discover them by serving in many areas.

Finally, look to your *church community* for affirmation. Don't underestimate the importance of having a local congregation of believers surrounding your life. As you head into the real world, you might be traveling a long distance from your home church. If that's the case, make sure you become involved in a congregation near your college. Get to know some people and begin to serve. Ask them what they think about your gifts, abilities, and passions. Chances are very good that as you serve, you'll talk about areas that are important to you and get you fired up. In this way your fellow church members could help you discover your major and future direction.

Tips for Exploring Your Major

As you apply these tips to discovering your major, consider some additional questions.[1] Take some time with God and journal your answers.

What do you really enjoy doing? (You could spend all day doing this. You love it.)

What can you do better than most people? (This isn't a prideful thing; just be honest.)

What would those who know you best say your greatest strengths are? (Ask them.)

Of the jobs listed here, which three are the most appealing to you and why? Accountant, fireman, computer programmer, nurse, mechanic, surgeon, farmer, lawyer, architect, flight attendant, astronomer, business executive, professor, teacher, policeman, engineer, scientist, dentist, paleontologist, statistician, psychiatrist, entrepreneur, salesman, therapist, doctor, contractor, real estate developer, writer, musician, pastor, youth pastor, missionary, actor/actress, yodeler, zoologist, politician, store owner, stockbroker, pilot, pharmacist, consultant.

What did you enjoy most about high school? ("Nothing" is not an answer.)

If money weren't an obstacle, what would you spend your time doing? (Again, "Nothing" is not an answer.)

---

[1] These questions were adapted from Sean Covey's *The Six Most Important Decisions You'll Ever Make* (Fireside, 2006).

If you could be famous for something, what would your
accomplishment be?

What needs do you see in the world that you'd like to help
meet?

What's God asking you to do?

Is there something you've always felt you should do with your
life but didn't have the courage to do?

These questions can lead you toward your major and other life
goals. You don't have to have it all figured out by tomorrow, but you
can't steer a parked car either. Start the car. Start serving. Start
listening to God's voice. Start paying attention to his movements
and the relationships he places in your life.

Timothy's "Major"

Timothy was a young man who traveled with Paul on missionary
journeys and sometimes stayed behind when Paul left to work with
other churches. Some scholars believe Paul might've led Timothy
to Christ, and Paul's last two letters before he died were written to
Timothy.

Paul's first letter to Timothy is filled with all kinds of good
advice. The aging apostle urged his young friend to "flee" evil and
"pursue righteousness, godliness, faith, love, endurance and gentleness" (1 Timothy 6:11). In other words, Paul told Timothy to run away
from bad stuff and run toward good stuff. Then he urged Timothy,
"Fight the good fight of the faith. Take hold of the eternal life to
which you were called when you made your good confession in the
presence of many witnesses" (6:12). That's good advice for Timothy
and every follower of Christ.

Paul offered similar words of challenge in his second letter to
Timothy: "But as for you, continue in what you have learned and
have become convinced of, because you know those from whom

you learned it" (2 Timothy 3:14). Paul told Timothy to follow Jesus for the long haul.

But it's in chapter 4 that Paul gives Timothy his calling. He tells him to "preach the word" and to "do the work of an evangelist" (2 Timothy 4:1–5). This was Timothy's major; he was to teach the world about Jesus Christ. If there had been seminaries or Bible colleges in his day, Timothy might have attended one to receive training. Paul helped Timothy discover a major that connected to his passions, gifting, natural talents, and desires.

You need a "Paul" or two who will help you as you take this journey of discovering your major. As Timothy went through a process of discovering the direction God was leading him in, he needed people who'd be willing to walk with him. The same is true for you. Don't try to go it alone.

Questions for the Journey

1. As you look ahead to college, are you excited about discovering your major? Or are you stressed?

2. What are the top-five things you like to do? How could these be connected to your major and life calling?

3. What steps can you take to help discover your major?

CHAPTER 12

Classroom: Maximizing Your Learning

Please pray I can maintain a Christlikeness in the university setting. There is so much disbelief. People say they're not religious, but I see they believe in themselves. The second day of geology class, a student tried to argue that creationism is true, and the class mocked him. I nudged him and told him the timing was not right. The professor said, "This is a science class, not a philosophy class." Later I asked the professor, "If it's not a philosophy class, then why do you believe in science?" He didn't have anything to say. I haven't been that nervous for a long time. I really need some ideas or input on how to live for Jesus in the college classroom.

—Jonathan, 22

Whoever dwells in the shelter of the Most High will rest in the shadow of the Almighty.

—Psalm 91:1

College Class Confrontation

The first quote above was taken from an email I received from a friend who was wrestling with the college classroom experience. He wrote to ask for prayer and encouragement, and I asked if he'd let me share the quote in this book. Why? It reveals the kind of classroom challenges you can experience in a secular university environment.

Pray for wisdom, asking God to show you the right path.

—David, 18

Know what you believe. Don't challenge your professors' authority, but stand by your understanding of God.

—Sally, 18

My friend Jonathan has it right: We all believe in someone or something. Depending on where you go to school, you may find yourself surrounded by professors and other students who will support and encourage you in your faith in Jesus, or you may feel like your beliefs are constantly being challenged. Either way, if you're a follower of Jesus who wants to make a difference at your college, this section is for you.

Wisdom 101

Everything starts in your mind. First Corinthians 8:1–2 says, "We know that 'We all possess knowledge.' But knowledge puffs up while love builds up. Those who think they know something do not yet know as they ought to know." Our actions consciously or subconsciously start in our minds. Whether we're choosing to do wrong or right, it's our brain that's first in play.

College can be a wonderful place on so many levels, but it's a place where knowing what you believe is very important. When you come to know the real Jesus, your mind has a different master teacher. Paul tells us we get a brand-new way of thinking when we become a follower of Jesus. He says, "Do not conform to the pattern of this world, but be transformed by the renewing of your mind. Then you will be able to test and approve what God's will is—his good, pleasing and perfect will" (Romans 12:2). This renewal of our minds starts with Jesus. Since Jesus is the same yesterday, today, and forever, we can depend on him for all wisdom and understanding (Hebrews 13:8–9). When you become a follower of Jesus, he's your pathway to true wisdom.

Proverbs tells us, "The fear of the LORD is the beginning of wisdom, and knowledge of the Holy One is understanding" (Proverbs 9:10). So wisdom starts with a healthy fear of God. What does this really mean? The fear this verse speaks of isn't a horror-movie kind of fear; rather, we should be in *awe* of God. The God of the universe is *awe*some. Understanding this is where true wisdom starts.

Good Judgment

In college you'll need to practice good judgment, which takes wisdom or discernment. When your English professor suggests you can never really know what an author meant by certain words, this should disturb your discernment radar. You begin to wonder: *Does that make sense? If I can't ever know what someone really means, then how do I know what this professor means when she speaks?* If your science professor says the material world is all that's out there—that what you can see, taste, touch, smell, and hear is all there is—you think to yourself, *Science says there was a beginning to the universe; and if there was a beginning, then there had to be a Creator of it all.* You might have a literature prof who views the Bible as just another book, or even a religion professor who sees the Bible as a purely human work. But then you begin to think about the verses you've studied that speak to the Scriptures being God-inspired and Spirit-guided, such as 2 Timothy 3:16 and 2 Peter 1:20–21.

Your discernment must be based on your growing relationship with God, your consistent study of Scripture, and the promise of the Holy Spirit guiding you to truth. Ask God to guide you. Stay on your toes. Listen closely to what your professors say and learn from them, but you should also understand that you don't have to believe everything they say.

Some students who've given their lives to Jesus find themselves at a crossroads of belief in certain college classrooms. Consider Susan, a young Christian who only recently made a decision to follow Jesus. She walks into her freshman philosophy class and encounters a professor who says the philosophy of the Bible is ignorant compared to other human philosophies. He seems to think human authority is more important than divine authority. Susan thinks to herself, *This professor is a tremendously intelligent person with a doctorate from an Ivy League university. He wrote the textbook that cost me an arm and leg to buy. Maybe he's right. I'm not sure I like everything in the Bible. Maybe I'd be better off as my own boss.*

> *There are a lot of college professors in the classroom who'll tell you everyone needs to figure out their own beliefs and everyone's beliefs are okay. This is a dangerous adventure if your core values aren't nailed down.*
>
> —Adam, 23

This is when a crisis of belief hits Susan like a ton of bricks. She's on her own now. She has total freedom from her parents and other authority figures. She feels she can't believe in both God's wisdom and her own wisdom. Worse yet, she feels she can't believe in both philosophy and Scripture. It's either this way or that. She wonders, *Is Jesus my Lord, or am I in charge?* As a result, Susan concludes that her philosophy professor is right. Her values are more important than God's.

This is a real situation that you may encounter in college, but it doesn't have to be a crisis of faith. Use your discernment in the classroom. Remember, just because many of your professors have doctorates and book credits and they're showing you "evidence" in class, that doesn't mean everything they say is true. Ask God to give you his wisdom and discernment to know the truth. Don't throw away your faith in Jesus because one professor says something that contradicts something you've learned from a parent or pastor.

The reality is all truth is God's truth. Jesus says, "I am the way and the truth and the life" (John 14:6). Each one of your professors was made by God and in God's image. Even if they're not followers of Christ, they're still able to speak God's truth. For instance, your physics professor might explain the theory of gravity. Scripture doesn't explain gravity in scientific terms, but it's still a truth: God set up the universe and created gravity. The important thing is to start with the truth of Scripture and let God guide you into the more detailed truth. Default to God and his Word over your professors' words—or your own!

In college (and throughout your life), it's important to surround yourself with smart and discerning people who possess depth of character and who love Jesus with all of their heart. These are people who might become mentors to you. (See chapter 19 on mentoring.) There are many Christians who've already walked the road you're walking. The issues you'll face in the college classroom are not new, and many people have been helped through these times by a community of intelligent Christ-followers. Martin Luther King Jr. said it best with the following words: "Intelligence plus character—that is the goal of a true education." A community of fellow disciples can help make sure your education is one that builds both intelligence and character.

Eight Steps to College Success

The first time you enter a college classroom, you'll immediately notice the differences from a high school class. For one thing, class sizes can vary dramatically. You may have some highly specialized classes with a dozen students or less, but other courses may have hundreds of students packed into the same lecture hall. Whatever the class size, here are a few suggestions to help you succeed in the classroom:

1. Get a laptop and take it to class with you. Hopefully you took a keyboarding class in high school. If you still have time, take it your senior year. I can't tell you how important it was for me to take a basic typing class. I was bored out of my mind, but it really paid off—today, I type on my computer all the time. You'll save time by typing your notes and organizing them later. Just don't spend class time playing games or emailing.

2. Take good notes. Maybe you were able to get through high school without having to take notes, but in college you'll have to learn to take effective notes if you want to do well. Listen carefully to what your professor says, but don't try to write down every word. Ask yourself, *Is this important to the professor? Is it likely to be on an exam or useful for a future paper or assignment?* If you can make friends with an upperclassman who took the class, you can ask them what your professor looks for in a good paper or what kinds of questions are on exams.

3. Take time after class to review your notes. This will save you time later. Instead of going back over your notes for the first time a day before the final exam, do little reviews after each class. This will keep the information in your brain longer. Right before bed is another great time to review your notes. Your brain will spend time with those thoughts all night, and you'll retain the information.

4. Make an effort to meet those you don't know in your classes, especially those who sit near you. Most of us are creatures of habit, so you'll probably sit in the same area for every class, and so will those around you. Who knows, you might meet a great lifelong friend (or a future spouse)!

5. Sit in the front row (or at least near the front of the class). I know you think I'm crazy on this one, but you'll learn more and pay better attention. Instead of looking at the backs of a dozen (or more) heads in the rows in front of you, you're better off sitting where your view is limited to the one who grades your papers.

6. Turn off your cell phone. There's nothing more distracting than a cell phone ringing, vibrating, or being typed on. You'll miss something important. Your friends can wait, even if they're sitting in the same class.

7. Arrive early to class. Don't be the one who tries to sneak in late—this won't sit well with your professor. Some professors even lock the door after a certain time. You're paying to take these classes, so go early and get your money's worth!

8. Don't check your brain at the classroom door. Be wise. Pay attention. Test everything. Is it from God or from another source? Is it true or false? There are times when you'll need to memorize something just to make the professor happy or to spit back some facts on a test. But most of the time you'll need to be discerning. Enjoy this stretching, challenging, and joyful time as you make choices to follow Jesus into the college classroom and beyond.

QUESTIONS FOR THE JOURNEY

1. How do you think the college classroom will compare to your high school classroom?

2. How do you intend to grow in wisdom while you're in college?

3. What's your game plan for discerning truth from error in the classroom lectures and reading?

4. How will you go about finding a trusted, Jesus-following friend to test what you learn?

CHAPTER 13

Money: Cash and Canned Goods

Keep your lives free from the love of money and be content with what you have, because God has said, "Never will I leave you; never will I forsake you."

— Hebrews 13:5

I'd like to live as a poor man with lots of money.

— Pablo Picasso

The Love of Money

Money. It's a strange thing. It can either cause great hope and encouragement, or great pain and heartache. The Benjamins have a way of shaping and driving you. Whether you're heading to college or a job in the real world, money will be a part of your life. Did you know that money can either hold you back or release you to do God's will for your life, depending on how you view and manage it? The Bible is clear: Money needs to be handled with extreme care. It says, "Whoever loves money never has enough; whoever loves wealth is never satisfied with their income" (Ecclesiastes 5:10). Money does not bring happiness, but it is a necessary part of adult life.

If money is used wisely, it has the ability to bless, encourage, give hope, and make a difference in many lives. It can be used to feed the hungry, provide wells for water around the world, or put a roof over your head. It's wise to hold money loosely, plan accordingly, and give it away joyfully.

Did you know the Bible has lots to say about how we handle our time and our gifts and abilities? It also has lots to say about how we take care of money, our treasure. It takes discipline, but our needs and our family's needs should come first. That might not sound correct, but the Bible says, "Anyone who does not provide for their relatives, and especially for their own household, has denied the faith and is worse than an unbeliever" (1 Timothy 5:8). *Wow!* Caring for those closest to us is most important. The way we use money for ourselves, for others, and especially for the sake of the kingdom of God is a spiritual issue.

Godliness and Gold

Our use of money and resources is critical to our spiritual growth. Sometimes we're motivated to live for God out of pure love for him, but other times it's just out of obedience. The Bible has so much to say about the use of wealth and possessions. If we get lazy and ignore living within our means and spending and investing wisely, then we aren't showing godliness. It's worth thinking about some biblical principles related to money.

First, *God* owns everything; *you don't.* Sometimes we think what we have is ours; but in reality, the Lord owns those jeans, that shirt, those boots, and that pair of khakis. "The earth is the LORD's, and everything in it" (Psalm 24:1; 1 Corinthians 10:26). That includes, well, *everything.* God owns it all. He tells Israel, "The whole earth is mine" (Exodus 19:5). And he declares in the book of Job, "Everything under heaven belongs to me" (Job 41:11).

We're just managers of God's creation. We are responsible to steward what he's given to us to take care of. If you have a car, it's

God's car. If you've been granted money to go to college, God allowed you to use it. The house, apartment, or dorm room you live in has God as its landlord. He is Lord of the land. God declares, "The silver is mine and the gold is mine" (Haggai 2:8). It is very important to start here. God owns it all. You don't. The question is not, *How much of my stuff should I give to God?* but rather, *How much of God's stuff should I keep for myself?* Meditate on this point. Let it sink deep into your heart. It will set the pace for how you view your stuff.

Second, since God owns it all, we should get in the habit of giving back some of what's his in the form of a tithe. Giving money back to God is a spiritual act of obedience and worship. There are biblical principles connected with financial offerings and the tithe (a tenth). This is another reason it's so important to be connected to a local church. It's a joyful act to give back to God for the work of ministry in the local church, for the glory of God, and for the good of the world.

Maybe you're thinking it would be too much sacrifice to tithe ten percent of what you have because you're a poor college student or have a low-paying job. Wait. Who provided the opportunity for you to go to college? Who gave you that job? Ultimately, it wasn't your hard work that paid off. It was God's blessing. If you believe God owns it all and if you're obedient to him, you will joyfully give in worship, ascribing worth back to God. This will be your first gift, not your last.

Third, giving reflects your faith that God will provide for you. God wants us to trust him with all of our lives. This includes our finances. There is a story in the Bible about a poor widow who was willing to give "all she had to live on" as her worship of Jesus (Mark 12:41–44). This doesn't mean we should all put all of our money in the offering plate, but it does mean we need to step out in faith and not let our money own us. Sometimes God calls us to give more than we think is possible as a demonstration of our faith in him and so we can watch him provide.

Fourth, giving should be generous and sacrificial. Many different Gallup polls show that believers in Jesus give on average only 2.8 percent of their income to the local church. Now, I know what you're going to say: "I don't have an income. I'm a poor college student," or "I just work at the little store on the corner, making minimum wage." It doesn't matter to God how much you put in the bank. It matters where your heart is. Are you a generous person? It isn't a sacrifice unless it's sacrificial. No one who gave generously and sacrificially for the purposes of God regretted it. God loves a cheerful giver. God doesn't want someone to give away their money with a grudging spirit, arms folded in disgust. Paul says, "Each of you should give what you have decided in your heart to give, not reluctantly or under compulsion, for God loves a cheerful giver" (2 Corinthians 9:7).

One man has said, "There are three kinds of giving: grudge giving, duty giving, and thanksgiving."[1] Believe it or not, God wants you to enjoy giving away your money for the kingdom.

Money Managing: The Checkbook

Let's get specific about heading into the real world with some money. I hope you already have a checking account and a savings account at a well-known bank. You might not have any money in these accounts, but at least you've opened them for the future.

With a checking account comes a checkbook. Let me give you three easy ways to destroy your checkbook balance (that is, the actual dollar amount in your bank). First, write checks or pay with a debit card like crazy, but never write the payments in your checkbook or watch your online expenses. Second, throw away your monthly bank statements like they're junk mail. Finally, use multiple checking accounts at once. These are three surefire ways to blow up your finances and become very frustrated when the bank calls because you don't have any money in your accounts.

Now, here are three easy ways to keep your checkbook balance intact. First, use your check register. It's that cute little paper ledger that came with your checks. It was free, so use it to record

---

[1] Quote is attributed to Robert N. Rodenmayer, *Thanks Be to God* (Harper, 1960).

the details of each check you write and every debit card purchase you make. A little time spent doing this along the way will save you hours of heartache later. Second, immediately subtract the check amount or add the deposit amount to your register balance. Pull out the old-fashioned calculator and get it done. Finally, when you receive your monthly statement from your bank (which you didn't throw away or delete from your inbox), check off each payment or debit, deposit or credit, and fee to make sure all the totals match. If there's an error, triple-check it. If the balance is still off, call your bank immediately. Not all bank statements are correct. Get in the habit of balancing your checkbook. It will save you time and give you joy in the long run.

Money Managing: The Food Budget

Whether you're headed to college, living at home, or living on your own and starting a new job, you have to eat. Maybe you've calculated the cost of eating in the college cafeteria and signed up for a meal plan with a certain number of meals. You still might want to buy groceries once in a while to keep things fun and fresh.

Here are some tips to cut your food budget. First, it might seem old-fashioned and like something your mom would do, but collect coupons. There are things called "double coupon days" where grocery stores help you save money. Do it. Second, take advantage of promos, discounts, and two-for-ones at local restaurants. Look for coupons online, and be sure to make eating out a special occasion, not a routine. Third, fast once in a while. Yes, the Bible talks about fasting as self-discipline. Do some research and go for it. Fourth, buy groceries from less trendy grocery stores and look for off-brand items. Fifth, shop with a friend and buy in bulk. Split the cost. Sixth, keep the recipes simple and without lots of crazy ingredients. Seventh, drink tap water. It's free. Eighth, making a batch of cookies from scratch is fun, but it costs more than buying a package of premade cookies. Keep it simple.

Six Steps to Budgeting

1. Figure out how much everything is going to cost, beginning with giving to the church.
2. Save all receipts for a month.
3. Divide receipts into categories like rent, utilities, food, entertainment, clothes, etc.
4. Compare the total monthly expense to the total monthly income.
5. If expenses are greater than income, look for ways to cut back.
6. If income is greater than expenses, look for ways to invest and save.

Repeat this procedure for a second month and then implement any necessary changes.

The Bible Gets the Final Word on Money

There are many good resources online and in books about how to manage your money well. Check them out. But the Bible also offers lots of sound financial advice from God. Meditate on these verses. How does this knowledge calm your fears about money matters? How do these verses challenge your thinking about money?

A good name is more desirable than great riches; to be esteemed is better than silver or gold. (Proverbs 22:1)

Those who trust in their riches will fall, but the righteous will thrive like a green leaf. (Proverbs 11:28)

The wicked borrow and do not repay, but the righteous give generously. (Psalm 37:21)

When a man makes a vow to the LORD or takes an oath to obligate himself by a pledge, he must not break his word but must do everything he said. (Numbers 30:2)

The rich rule over the poor, and the borrower is slave to the lender. (Proverbs 22:7)

You will be enriched in every way so that you can be generous on every occasion, and through us your generosity will
result in thanksgiving to God. (2 Corinthians 9:11)

A generous person will prosper; whoever refreshes others will
be refreshed. (Proverbs 11:25)

Be careful that no one entices you by riches; do not let a large
bribe turn you aside. (Job 36:18)

Has your perspective on money changed? Did you have a biblical view before you read this chapter? Does the way you get and
give money reflect your relationship with Jesus? It isn't too late to
plan to use your money for the glory of God. As you begin this great
adventure with God—whether heading off to college or getting a
job—be wise with your wealth. In Christ, you really are rich. He's
given you many blessings that you can give back to him in worship.
Start with your checkbook.

QUESTIONS FOR THE JOURNEY

1. How important is money to you? Does it drive you? Do you
   wish it didn't exist?
2. What's the most challenging part of this chapter for you? Why?
3. What's your plan for managing your money as you head into the
   real world?
4. Where can you cut spending in order to save money?
5. Where can you give your money away to bless others?

CHAPTER 14

Stress: Managing the Pressure

My family life puts a lot of stress on me. My parents recently got divorced, and it took a huge toll on me. Life at home can get crazy, and sometimes I lose sight of God. Problems with and between my friends also stress me out. It seems there's always one problem or another, and it would just be nice to have some peace.

—Jaclyn, 17

Since we have been justified through faith, we have peace with God through our Lord Jesus Christ.

—Romans 5:1

Pressure and Peace

If there's one thing that almost everyone in their late teens and twenties has in common, it's that six-letter word. I'll give you a hint: It starts with S and rhymes with *mess*. Do you know it? It's S-T-R-E-S-S.

According to a survey in *Advertising Age*, 41 percent of twenty-somethings say they feel either quite a bit of pressure or almost more stress than they can bear. When I started to write this book,

I sent out a questionnaire to more than 100 young people. I asked them what things in their lives were causing stress. Here are just a few of their responses:

Money
Jobs
Housing
School
Relationships
Disappointing my parents
Not sleeping
Sports
Acceptance
Picking the right friends
Staying friends
Sinning
Trying to keep up with everything
What will happen after high school
Using my time wisely
Being bored
Myself

> *I take time to rest and relax by sitting on the couch and snuggling in a blanket while watching a good movie. Sometimes you need to just get away from all the hectic stuff in life.*
>
> —Jodi, 15

This list has kept me praying for those young people and for all of you who are reading this book during this transitional time in your life. But the very last word on that list concerns me the most. When the pressure is on—when all of those other areas are pushing in on you—it can be hard to look in the mirror and not be stressed about what you see. That's one of the reasons I wrote this book and why the first section is on identity. When you know who you are and what you believe, when you place your faith in Christ and foster intimacy with Jesus, the peace of God sits deep in your heart. That doesn't mean you'll never face times of stress and difficulty. You will. But because of your relationship with Jesus, peace will dwell in your heart. You'll have an inner confidence that God is in control of your life. That kind of deep peace with God offers you calm and security that can sustain you regardless of the circumstances.

Good News

When I think about this kind of peace, I often reflect on a scene from Scripture that's usually connected to Christmas. It's possible you're reading this book during the heat of the summer. If so, you might want to pause and make yourself a cup of hot cocoa, just to get in the Christmas spirit. Go ahead, I'll wait.

Rest and relaxation are so important. There are times when I just need to be by myself and escape into nature. At other times, being with others and having a great laugh is enough to bring life back into my worn-out body.

—Ryan, 24

Now go with me to a hillside where shepherds watch their sheep. Get into the shepherds' sandals for a few minutes. Feel the breeze on your face. Listen to the *baas* of the sheep. Look down toward the city of Bethlehem nearby.

Then—POOF! Out of nowhere an angel appears in front of you with a most surprising message: "Do not be afraid!" *Are you kidding?* you think. *Of course I'm afraid! You're an angel, and I don't see angels every day. As a matter of fact, I've never seen an angel.* But the angel continues, "I bring you good news that will cause great joy for all the people. Today in the town of David a Savior has been born to you; he is the Messiah, the Lord. This will be a sign to you: You will find a baby wrapped in cloths and lying in a manger" (Luke 2:10–12).

You and the other shepherds look at one another, wondering if you can really believe what you just saw and heard. *Amazing! What does this mean? The long-awaited Messiah has come. In that city? Really? The Messiah? The One who will finally rescue all of us?*

Then, SLAM! BAM! Now a multitude (that's a lot) of angels appear, and they begin singing, "Glory to God in the highest heaven, and on earth peace to those on whom his favor rests" (10:14). It gets even better. Peace has come. The angels leave, you pick your jaw up off the ground, grab your crook, and head for Bethlehem to see the Messiah—the Prince of Peace. When you finally get there and see

Jesus, you're so astonished that you run out the door to tell everyone (Luke 2:15–17)!

I think this familiar story with its message of peace has some lessons we can use year-round to tackle the stress in our lives.

First, realize that peace is a gift from God. The angels announced this good news to the shepherds. The peace announcement has been given to you too. The coming of the Messiah offers the promise of inner peace to every human, as well as an end to warring between nations.

> *I just hang out with my Christian friends, and I use that time to get relaxed and refocused.*
>
> —Suzie, 18

Second, the story tells us peace should be pursued with passion. The shepherds didn't sit around after the angelic rock concert and say, "Well, that was nice, but I wish they'd had a little more drum." No, they hurried off to see the Savior. We can't sit and whine in our stress. The writer of Psalms says it clearly: "Seek peace and pursue it" (Psalm 34:14).

Third, it's the Messiah who offers peace. When the shepherds arrived at the side of the cradle, looked into baby Jesus's eyes, and touched his fragile hands, I imagine their hearts melted. I believe they surrendered to the Prince of Peace in that moment. We also need to make peace with the Messiah on an ongoing basis. Scripture tells us "we have peace with God through our Lord Jesus Christ" (Romans 5:1).

Fourth, the story tells us this peace isn't meant for us alone, but it must be passed on to the rest of the planet. You're probably not the only one who's stressed out about the circumstances of life. There are others whose situations are worse than yours. As a matter of fact, there are many who face stress without Jesus to help them through the tough times. They don't know the Prince of Peace. It's our job to partner with God and tell them this story. The shepherds were the first evangelists on the planet. They ran off to tell the world about Jesus. We should too.

> *I spend alone time with God to get refreshed by enjoying God's creation.*
>
> —Justine, 17

Fifth, this peace is worth praising

God. The shepherds gave us a model: They returned to glorify God and praise Jesus for his birth. They remained in awe of this whole event. Worship has a way of helping us cope with the stress around us. When you're dealing with difficulty, work up the courage to sing new songs to the Lord. Make some joyful noise to the King of kings.

> *When I'm alone, I can just belt out my praises or requests to God.*
>
> —Haylee, 15

Handling Depression

What if there's more to this stress? It's no secret that high school and the years that follow are a time when many people fall into depression. According to the Teen Health & Wellness website (*teenhealthandwellness.com*), suicide is the third-leading cause of death among people ages fifteen to twenty-four in the United States. Depression is a very serious problem. Don't be fooled: Even those who love Jesus can struggle with depression.

Maybe you feel like your problems are so overwhelming that you don't know what to do. Perhaps you think you're stupid for even feeling this way. There is hope, but you can't do it alone.

Many who suffer from depression choose to keep it to themselves, believing they can fight their way through it alone. They're trying to build their own life preservers even as they feel themselves drowning in the open sea. This is no time to be silent. This is the time to yell for help. Go! Run! Hurry! Choose a close and trusted friend, pastor, sibling, parent, step-parent, grandparent, professor, physician, coach, teacher, or counselor to talk to. And if the first person you tell doesn't take you seriously, keep searching until you've found a trusted friend who does.

Don't worry about looking dumb or needy. Sometimes depression has its roots in biology, plain and simple. And sometimes it has its roots in deep and abiding pain. Whatever your case may be, it's critical that you address it with the support of those who love you. We were built for community and connection with others. And remember: Jesus will always be there with you, even as you walk through this valley of shadows. Jesus walked through the same valley just hours before he was nailed to the cross for our sins (Luke 22:39–46). Here's the good news: If there's a valley, then there must be a mountaintop. No matter how difficult it might seem, victory is yours through Jesus Christ who conquered death.

A Place of Tranquility

In 1969 U.S. astronauts landed on the moon for the first time. (I know—that was before you were born. It happened before I was born too.) After the lunar module Eagle landed on the moon, the astronauts set up what would be called Tranquility Base. It was an ironic name for the site of such a daring and dangerous mission.

Did you know that when the crew of Apollo 11 landed the lunar module, they had less than a minute of fuel remaining? In fact, some scientists estimate there were only eleven seconds worth of fuel left! Eleven seconds! Can you believe it? And they performed that whole moon mission with less computer power than I have in my minivan! NASA seemed to be communicating a biblical principle: You can have peace in the midst of stress.

Oceanographers say that no matter how high the ocean waves might be at any particular moment, the sea is always tranquil and peaceful twenty feet below the surface. No matter how bad the storm rages on top of the ocean, the waters are calm down deep. The believer in Jesus finds peace in the same place—down deep! Shallow belief in Jesus leaves you anxious and fearful when the storms rise, but deep, stable faith in Jesus provides tranquility in the midst of severe and threatening storms.

One of the most important things you can do when you're feeling stressed is gain perspective. Step back and look at what you're facing in light of the big picture. Then go buy a grande Caramel Macchiato from Starbucks and drink it in a hammock. Exercise like crazy. Pray without ceasing. Run a lap. Play soft music. Take large, overwhelming tasks and break them down into bite-sized pieces. Buy a punching bag. Sit in a hot tub. Light some candles. Say no to something. You get the picture.

On the other hand, there are some things you *shouldn't* do while attempting to deal with stress. If you're stressed, don't bite your fingernails, get drunk, try to do everything all at once, take pills, drive crazy, eat a whole quart of ice cream, fill your calendar so full you can't breathe, punch your roommate (even if you say you're doing it "in Jesus's name"), play in the road, or put firecrackers in your mouth and light them. These aren't good ideas. Don't do them.

I want to end this chapter on a more serious note—and one that will give you some hope when the stress is real. Paul gave the Christians in Corinth (and all followers of Jesus) a great reminder that even when times get difficult, we should not lose heart: "We are hard pressed on every side, but not crushed; perplexed, but not in despair; persecuted, but not abandoned; struck down, but not destroyed" (2 Corinthians 4:8–9).

Let me put it another way: You might feel like a quarterback being rushed by a whole gang of linebackers, but you'll never be sacked. Every now and then you might feel like a rubber band stretched to your max, but you won't break. There are even times when you'll feel like a boxer being beaten, bruised, and thrown against the ropes repeatedly, but you won't be knocked out.

Why? Because "we always carry around in our body the death of Jesus, so that the life of Jesus may also be revealed in our body" (2 Corinthians 4:10). Like jars of clay (2 Corinthians 4:7), we're fragile and breakable on the outside, but filled with the rock-solid strength of Jesus.

So we don't lose heart. We don't give up or give in to stress. We mature as we follow Jesus.

QUESTIONS FOR THE JOURNEY

1. What stresses you out?
2. Do you feel like your life is coming together or falling apart?
3. How has God used stressful moments to shape the person you're becoming?
4. What are some good habits you can develop to combat stress as you follow Jesus?

PART THREE

Belonging—
Where Do I Fit?

Your brothers and sisters in Christ are your support group, your true friends. They'll stand with you no matter what, and they'll help bring you back if you ever fall away. They're your anchor, your life raft, your survival kit, part of your fit on earth; you can't make it through the hostile waters of life without them. They're invaluable.

—Shae, 18

As you long for freedom from your parents, as you long to get out on your own, there's this voice inside of you yelling, *Let me out of here! I'm my own person!* The world affirms this demand. From music to television to movies, the message gets repeated again and again: "It's all about ME."

Elsewhere in this book we've talked about how important it is to discover your design, to realize the unique person God created you to be. But that doesn't mean you're meant to go it alone. You were designed for connection, for relationship with others. Jesus affirms the importance of connection over and over again through all of the "one another" ideas in his teachings: Love one another, serve one another, bear one another's burdens, forgive one another, and many more.

We know we're connected to other stories—not only God's story, but also the stories of those around us. Whenever someone says, "Wow, it's a small world," we can be sure that person has just discovered another connection. We're pieces of an amazing puzzle that God has assembled.

Think of your friends—in high school, in college, or on the job. You love them, care for them, and would probably die for them. You already understand the importance of these connections. You know we were made not just for individual stuff, but also together stuff. So you're looking for freedom but longing for community. This is called **interdependence**. It can be a difficult tension inside of you—a constant push-and-pull between "me" and "us."

In this section we'll walk through places of belonging, starting with your parents and moving through the other key connections in your life. My prayer is that you'll discover new ways in which your relationships can help you become a fully mature, Jesus-following adult.

CHAPTER 15

Parents: Adjusting Your Relationship

Leaving home was a good thing for my relationship with my parents because I learned to value them more. It changes when you get older. You learn that your parents have desires and passions outside of you. I make it a point to know them and understand them. I'm starting to value so much my parents' advice and opinions, but I'm also learning that I'm a separate person and that I'm responsible for myself and for seeking the Lord's will in my life, not necessarily my mom's will.

—Annie, 29

Honor your father and your mother, so that you may live long.

—Exodus 20:12

From Small to Big

When each one of my three children was born, there was a natural connection between my wife and the newborn child. It only makes sense. Laurie carried those kids in her body for nine months, gave birth to them, and nursed them. I don't mean to minimize the importance of dads or the strong connection between my kids and me. But it never surprised me that when baby Lillian, Levi, or

Lara would begin to cry, the one they really seemed to want was their mommy. This is the way God's economy works.

> *Hang out with your parents more and let them into your life. Instead of hanging out with friends, ask your parents to go see a movie, or just hang out with them at home.*
>
> —Candice, 17

But as a child grows and becomes a teenager, the attachment to one's parents changes. As kids grow more independent, they want to be in control. That desire often leads to conflict.

Think back to your last argument with your mom or dad. What was the argument about? What was it *really* about? It probably had something to do with you striving for independence and gaining control while still doing your best to gain their trust.

This is all natural. As you make the transition from adolescence into adulthood, you'll probably feel some tension from your mom and dad. It's difficult for them to let go. There's also tension on your end because you want them to let go. This can lead to a major tug of war. Understanding the tensions that surround this transition can help you better understand some of your parents' "crazy" behavior.

Parenting is a tough job. Hopefully your parents have been able to do the five things mentioned in Mr. Chap and Dee Clark's book, *Disconnected*,[1] during your middle and high school years.

First, I hope they've offered you understanding. This doesn't mean they always agree with you or they like your words and actions all the time. But hopefully you know they love you no matter what you do.

Second, I hope your parents have shown you compassion. There might have been times when your mom and dad wanted to get closer to you, but you felt suffocated and pulled away. It's natural for you to desire to be more independent, but that can be hard on your parents. Hopefully, they've showed you real compassion as you've sought greater independence.

---

[1] Baker, 2007.

Third, I hope your parents set boundaries for you so you had a safe balance between being fully alive and completely dead. I hope they love Jesus so much they want you to wholeheartedly love him too. So they set up rules to help you move in the right direction. And I hope these boundaries were full of grace.

Fourth, I hope your parents offered you guidance. I hope your parents charted the course and helped you along your journey. This doesn't mean they should choose your college or decide whom you should marry, but I do hope they help you find your direction and avoid rough terrain. Believe it or not, most parents have protected their children from many unnecessary scrapes and bruises throughout their lives.

Fifth and finally, as you'll soon make this transition to college and your independent life, I hope your parents will be able to let go. After being the ones who've held your hand every time you crossed the street, I hope your parents have been able to release that hand, give you a hug, and let you set sail for adulthood. I hope they're your biggest fans for following after Jesus.

Understanding, compassion, boundaries, guidance, and letting go—those are five essential gifts parents can give their children. None of us is perfect, and I'm sure your parents haven't handled every situation exactly the way you wish they had. But if your parents have been able to offer you these things throughout most of your life, you've been blessed. Give them a call to say thanks.

What If They Didn't?

Unfortunately, not everyone has a healthy relationship with his or her parents. I'm not talking about little conflicts that drive every teenager crazy. I'm talking about serious stuff.

I made an intentional shift in my relationship with my parents when I left high school. It's going to be different for everyone. I wouldn't recommend cutting your parents loose as soon as you graduate; you'll quickly find out all the things they've been doing for you that have made your life easier.

—Adam, 23

I hope your relationship with your parents has been a healthy one. But if it hasn't—if you've been neglected, abandoned, or suffered from physical or sexual abuse—let me tell you how deeply sorry I am. It wasn't fair to you. It wasn't what God wanted for you. But there's hope. The psalmist offers encouragement for those who've been mistreated or abandoned when he declares God is the "father to the fatherless" (Psalm 68:5). God can make up the difference in your life even if one or both of your parents weren't honoring God in their parenting of you.

> *My relationship with my parents improved after high school. The first time I was sick at college and called home, I realized just how much I really missed my mom. I could see on my parents' faces how hard it was for them to move me in to my new college dorm room and then drive away.*
>
> *— Tammy, 28*

Now let me say something else that might feel incredibly difficult if you're facing such a situation. For the sake of your own emotional and spiritual health, I would urge you to try to forgive your parents. I know it won't be easy—and maybe it can't happen immediately. But as you make the transition into adulthood, if your parents have fallen short in any of the tasks I mentioned earlier, offer them as much grace as you can. Don't hold it against them. Some of you might have a hard time with my words here, but God's desire is for forgiveness and health for you and your parents. God wants you to be whole, and I believe the path to wholeness, as difficult as it may seem, is a journey of forgiveness, release, and love.

Relationships Change

I probably don't need to tell you that relationships change over time (though I just did). You might not believe this today, but the people who've been your closest friends during the last three or four years may not be the people you stay the closest to for the rest of your life. I remember thinking that some of my high school buddies would be great friends of mine for the rest of my life. Can I be honest? This may shock you, but nearly twenty years later, I don't even know where many of them are.

Your relationship with your parents will change as well. They will always be your mom and dad; but now, instead of being the people who ground you for the weekend or allow you to go to the movies, they can become your good friends. That's right: Your mom and dad can become your close friends as you make this transition. It's strange but true: These people who've had so much to say about your life up until this point are also making a transition. They should be loosening their grip and becoming friends with you too.

> *I've maintained a good relationship with my parents by spending quality time with them. Sometimes I say no to friends who want to hang out so I can chill with my parents. You have to make time to talk with them and hang out if you want to keep a healthy relationship.*
>
> — Stephanie, 18

From the time you were born, your relationship with your parents has been evolving—and it's in the process of changing once again. As a child, you were very dependent on them. Today, you're becoming much less dependent, but hopefully you're still very connected.

Take some time to think about what a God-centered friendship with your mom and dad would look like. How could you bring approval and acceptance to them? How could you show your love to them as you near graduation and head into adulthood?

Honor Roll

Paul offered the church in Ephesus many tips for following after Jesus in households. Hidden away in a few verses are the expectations for children. Even though you're not a five-year-old anymore, you're still your parents' child. Paul says, "Children, obey your parents in the Lord, for this is right. 'Honor your father and mother'— which is the first commandment with a promise—'so that it may go well with you and that you may enjoy long life on the earth'" (Ephesians 6:1–3).

Paul reminds us that back when God gave Moses the Ten Commandments, the commandment to honor our parents also included a reason: so that you'll have a long and rewarding life. In other words, if you honor your mom and dad, God's blessings of peace, love, joy, and the like will be yours. There's a deep connection between your spiritual health and your attitude toward your parents.

> *I don't keep anything bundled up inside with my parents. I lay it all on the table so there are no regrets later.*
>
> —Jodi, 15

But what does *honor* mean? Have you been on the honor roll at school? Does an honor guard sound familiar? Honor is displayed when you lift people up, respect them, love them, put them before yourself, celebrate them, and show the world you care for them.

Becoming a good friend to your parents starts with honoring them. Celebrate the fact that they changed your diapers, taught you to ride a bike, helped you with countless hours of homework, went to your sporting events, and maybe even helped you buy your first car (and covered the cost of auto insurance). Think of all the great qualities they have—make a list.

But don't keep these things to yourself. Plan a "date" with your mom and dad to tell them how valuable they are to you. If you're still in high school, plan this date before you leave for college. If you've already made the transition to college or moved out, plan the date for a time when you're home or on break. After this first date, enjoy the benefits and blessings of more dates as you grow in your friendship with those who raised you.

Starting Fresh

Before I end this chapter, let me ask you something: Do your parents know you? This might seem like a silly question but think about it. It's quite possible that you went through your high school years feeling like your parents never really understood who you are. Am

I right? There might have been days (and late nights) when you tried your best to express to your parents what was going on with you—your greatest needs, your biggest stresses, your deep faith in Jesus—but you weren't sure they got it. Maybe you felt like you and your parents were speaking two different languages.

Maybe your parents haven't always taken the quality and quantity of time necessary to really know you as an emerging adult. But let's put that aside for a minute and turn the tables. Think about the question the other way around: Do you really know your parents?

Here's a series of questions to help you consider how well you know your mom and dad. Most of the questions can apply equally well to either parent. If you know the answer to these questions, that's awesome! If you don't, this might be a great list of things for you to talk about on your upcoming date with them.[2]

What color are your mom's eyes?

What is your dad's favorite thing to do?

What would your parents say is the nicest thing you could do for them?

If your mom and dad had all the time and money in the world, what would they spend their time doing?

What are their views on marriage?

What do your mom and dad think about Jesus?

What is your dad's greatest unfulfilled dream?

What place in the world would your mom most like to visit?

What was your dad's first full-time job?

What does your mom remember about the major world events she's lived through?

Where did your parents first meet?

---

[2] This list of questions was adapted from Sean Covey's *The Six Most Important Decisions You'll Ever Make* (Fireside, 2006).

Who's your dad's closest friend?

What's your mom's favorite kind of music?

What were their favorite television shows when they were children?

Whom did your parents vote for in the last election? Why?

Does your dad fill up the car's gas tank when it's half-empty or does he wait until the last possible moment?

What's your mom's favorite place to eat?

How did you do? No matter how well you did on this exercise, keep striving to know your parents better and really discover what it means to become adult friends with them. This new relationship has the potential to challenge you, stretch you, and take you deeper with Jesus. Take advantage of building beautiful friendships with your parents.

QUESTIONS FOR THE JOURNEY

1. How is your relationship with your parents today? What are some areas in which it could improve?
2. How will your parents and family feel about your transition to college and the life ahead of you? What will be the most difficult aspect for them?
3. How do you feel about leaving home?
4. In what practical ways can you honor your parents?

CHAPTER 16

Friends: Finding and Keeping Them

A good friend is a person who is there with you when it's good and when things go bad. They are someone who will help you grow in Christ and care enough about you to tell you when you shouldn't be doing something.

—Stephanie, 18

Walk with the wise and become wise,
for a companion of fools suffers harm.

—Proverbs 13:20

The Purple Dinosaur

Barney drives me crazy. You know who I'm talking about: The purple dinosaur on PBS. For some odd reason, children seem mesmerized by this guy in a big purple suit and his dance moves. But I don't get it.

I was introduced to this creature—part giant stuffed animal, part purple pillow—back when my oldest nephew was a young child. He's in college now, and, to my amazement, *Barney and Friends* is still incredibly popular with little kids. Over the years countless children (including mine, until we banned Barney from our house) have sat in front of the TV screen spellbound, or have sung and danced along with Barney and his not-so-purple pals. Maybe the songs on the show have a positive message; but whenever I hear them, I just want to yell, "Stop watching! This isn't good for your health!"

But there's another Barney who's very real, and his ideas about friendship are very good for your spiritual health. His full name was Barnabas. And like many other characters in the Bible, his name summed up who he was. The name *Barnabas* means "encourager"—and that's exactly what Barnabas was. He came alongside the apostle Paul with unconditional love and support. He was a good friend. Barnabas introduced the rest of the disciples to Paul because he believed in him. Paul experienced difficult times, but Barnabas represented, defended, and supported him in the midst of criticism. That's what good friends do.

There are many other scriptural examples of deep friendships, such as Jonathan and David, or Ruth and Naomi. Ruth's care for and commitment to Naomi was so deep that she once said, "Where you go I will go, and where you stay I will stay. Your people will be my people and your God my God" (Ruth 1:16). And Jonathan was so loyal that he protected David even when Jonathan's own father, King Saul, wanted David killed. The Bible says, "Jonathan became one in spirit with David, and he loved him as himself" (1 Samuel

I have a handful of very close friends. They're people who share my beliefs and make it a point to understand and care about my passions. These people are my lifeblood, and I share with them, not only because it blesses me, but also because it blesses them. I value their opinions very much. I also have friends in my life who are social friends, who I hang out with and have just dumb conversation with. We laugh and have fun, but there's not much depth to them; we just have a lot in common. Then there are friends that I'm close to, but only because I know a lot about what's going on in their life. These are people that don't take a vested interest in me, but I know I'm in their life, perhaps to enrich them or pray for them. This works for me because I have people at the other end of the spectrum enriching me.

—Lori, 29

18:1). I think we all long for this kind of deep friendship—even if we're not used to talking that way. (Don't worry, guys. I'm sure they high-fived each other at times.)

Facts about Friends

Long ago the Greek philosopher Aristotle said, "Without friends no one would choose to live." I think he's right on the money. Christ is the center of our lives, but good friendships are essential for the mature, Jesus-following adult. We were built for community—that's why God didn't leave Adam alone in the garden for long. First there was Adam, then Eve, and humans continued to fulfill God's command to reproduce. Need I say more?

> *A good friend is someone who lets me be vulnerable but who's also willing to be vulnerable with me. A good friend is someone who prays, listens, cries, challenges, and just stays silent. A good friend knows when you're operating out of hurt and desires to bring you home.*
>
> —Sara, 29

So what does it mean to be a good friend? Here are five suggestions to help keep your friendships healthy and strong as you follow Jesus:

1. Friends provide a shield. They don't leave you vulnerable. To be a good friend involves some healthy and godly protection. Friends look out for each other. They keep each other out of danger and hold each other accountable. Friends have each other's backs.

2. Friends are faithful. A good friend doesn't run away when times get tough. Friends say things like, "I'm here for you no matter what" and mean it. If a difficult and stressful event happens in your friendship, you stay in the fight (or discussion). Friends don't walk away.

3. Friends tell the truth. They don't lie or fake it. Telling the truth requires wisdom and courage. The truth needs to be told at the right time, in the right way, and to the right people. We can't run from it even if it's hard. If you love your friend, you'll be willing to tell the truth even when it's difficult.

4. Friends don't point fingers. Good friends ask questions; they don't place blame. If you're selfless, thinking of your friend as better than yourself, you won't accuse him of anything. Ask questions of clarity, but don't point fingers. Friends don't draw conclusions until they have all the facts.

5. Friends make the extra effort. They're intentional about making the first move toward reconciliation. They value the other person more than themselves. They love with patience and care, just as Paul explained to the Corinthian church in 1 Corinthians 13.

Types of Friends

All of us intuitively know there are different types of friends. Some people have more friends than others (especially on Facebook), but not all of our friends are on the same level of connection. Your friends might include both the woman who works at the grocery store checkout that you say hi to once a week, as well as the person you've known all your life and share your deepest secrets with. It's important to be aware of what stage your various friendships are in so you treat them with the proper amount of intimacy.

There are people you meet at the mall or at the movies. These are people you happen to stumble across who don't influence your life very much. You might run into one such friend some evening and not see him again for months. But the funny thing about God is that he'll sometimes take a casual friend like this and, over time, turn him or her into a person you'd die for. Just pay attention and stay alert to God's movement.

> *My closest friends are the ones that I can share with on a spiritual level. They'll listen to me in my darkest, dirtiest moments and still be my friend. They're the ones I know I can call at any time, having full confidence they'll make time for me. I know I can call my best friend, Ryan, and tell him I need a place to stay for the weekend and he would make it happen. These kinds of friends are usually not made overnight, but over a good amount of time.*
>
> *— Sam, 23*

There are also friends you hang with. As you move from high school to college or a career, your friendships will change. The people you hung out with in high school might feel more distant when you no longer see them every day. But you'll develop new connections with people you feel safe with. Give these friends permission to speak into your life when you're high and low.

> *A good friend is someone who knows my heart, dreams, and passions. They also know my struggles and failures, yet love me and accept me completely, both the good and the bad.*
>
> —Ryan, 24

Then there's a smaller group of friends you really trust. When you have secrets to tell, this is the group you express them to. The closer you get to one another, the more vulnerable you are with them. The more you care about them, the more potential there is to be hurt by them. This is the group you laugh the hardest with and weep the longest with. There is deep trust.

Finally, over the course of your life, you might have a few special friends with whom you feel the closest. You'd do anything for these people. These friends believe in you, and you believe in them. Nothing can get in the way of your love for these people. They're like food and air to your soul. Go further with them. Pray longer with and for them. Keep things that are shared between you and these friends confidential. These friends are precious—so love, foster trust with, and believe in them.

Friendship was God's design. If it's true that we all have a hole in our hearts that only God can fill, then there are also human-sized holes that need to be filled. We have only so much time, energy, and room for friendships. So choose your friends wisely, and you'll reap huge rewards.

Handling Conflict

Sometimes you'll experience conflict in your friendships. If you don't ever have conflict, then you don't have friends. Friends care enough to confront one another, and they care enough to be hurt by one another.

Learning how to handle conflict is essential. If it's not handled properly, then conflict can deeply damage a person or relationship. Some people actually enjoy conflict (at least initially), while others run from it like they're fleeing a burning home. Which way do you respond to conflict? Do you fight or take flight? Do you become aggressive or retreat? Do you demand that it be resolved right now, or do you hide your feelings like nothing happened? Understanding your own reactions is the first step to facing conflict.

> *My closest friends would be the ones that I can tell anything to, trust with everything, and know that they'll have my back no matter what. My closer friends would be the ones I have a good relationship with, but I may not always tell them everything on my mind or trust them with certain things. My close friends would be ones that I enjoy being around, but I probably wouldn't tell them much and I couldn't be around them all the time.*
>
> —Jaclyn, 17

Next, you need to understand the person you're in conflict with. Find a time to address the conflict with them face to face. Be willing to give each other time and space to cool down, collect your thoughts, and pray. Then, with mutual love and respect, pray and talk it out. Use "I felt" statements to talk about your own experience of the situation, not accusing "you" statements that criticize or place blame. Once you've discussed the problem and worked it out, decide (out loud) to forgive one another and put it behind you. This is hard, but keep practicing. Over time, this will help you grow closer to one another and to God.

> *A good friend is someone who I can share anything with and not be written off. A good friend doesn't ditch me for an activity or relationship.*
>
> —Joe, 22

There's no single, universal formula for conflict resolution. Matthew 18:15–20 suggests some principles to follow when sin is clearly involved, but often the question of whether or not someone has sinned is part of the conflict. Of course, much conflict comes from pride, jealousy, envy, selfishness, and desire for control—and God is not honored by these motivations.

Always ask yourself, *What am I learning about myself in this conflict?* Stay humble and teachable. This will get you well on your way to developing deeper friendships and growing in your relationship with Jesus.

QUESTIONS FOR THE JOURNEY

1. What you are the qualities of a good friend?
2. How have you been a good friend to others?
3. How is your relationship with God like a friendship?
4. When difficult times come, who will walk beside you as you make this transition?

CHAPTER 17

Dorm Life: Bonding With Strangers

Meet as many different people as you can, and get involved with a good group of believers in Jesus.

—Ally, 22

Now that you have purified yourselves by obeying the truth so that you have sincere love for each other, love one another deeply, from the heart.

—1 Peter 1:22

Surviving

Have you ever been dropped onto an island with strangers? Think of the long-running television show *Survivor*, but you aren't *necessarily* trying to outwit, outplay, and outlast your fellows, voting them off the island at the end of the show. If you are reading this chapter, then you're either deciding whether or not to live in a dorm, are living in a dorm, or are headed toward a dorm on a college campus. Dorm life can feel a little like being placed on an island with strangers, but you do get to leave the "island" every day if you choose.

Dorm life can be an amazing opportunity to form lifelong

friendships, laugh, work through conflict, and build your character. You will learn a lot about those around you and also discover what makes you tick. There will be things you like about dorm life and things you'll be glad you had to experience only for a short time.

A dorm is more than simply a place to sleep and keep your stuff. It is also a "laboratory" where you'll find your college community. It's amazing how in your first few weeks of college, some people living in the dorm—including your roommate(s)—can become great friends almost overnight.

Maybe you're a little fearful of what's about to happen to you. This chapter will offer you some help in navigating dorm life. I want to give you some creative, practical, and necessary ideas for the journey.

Dorm Life

Living in the dorm can be a blast. You will laugh a lot, stay up all night cramming for that final or writing that paper, enjoy deep conversations, be tested on multiple levels, and negotiate relationships. Let me give you some practical tips for making the most of your time in this little community.

Add a little creative touch to your dorm room door. Many who live in the dorm will decorate their entry doors with pictures, borders, dry-erase boards for friends to leave notes, and random quotes connected with their personalities.

Take the initiative to start a small group or Bible study on your dorm floor. Have the meetings in your room. Maybe this scares you because you've never taken the lead with a small group—especially one centered around the Bible. Don't worry. Go for it. This is a great way to meet new people and build friendships around what God thinks. If you're attending a secular university or college, step out in faith and ask if folks would like to discuss God using the Bible. Who knows? You might help someone come to know Jesus as his or her Savior. Just have fun with this adventure.

Hang out in the common room sometimes. Dorms typically have a common area where everyone seems to hang out when they're bored, studying, or watching television. Even with the TV on, it's a great place to get to know people and find out who the like-minded friends will be. Take advantage of this. Oftentimes full dorm meetings will take place there. There might even be a pool table or Ping-Pong table to gather around in the name of competitive fun.

Get involved in the dorm activities. Often there are dorm committees that organize get-togethers for the dorm dwellers. They might be formed around holidays, sports, or just food and fellowship. The first few weeks of school are a good time to get really involved in these activities.

Wear flip-flops in the shower. (If you have a community bathroom, that is.) There are lots of things left on the shower floor that you don't want your feet to touch. That's all I will say about that.

Decorate your dorm room the way you want to. Of course, you'll need to show sensitivity to your roommate and the rules of the school, but mark your territory with some style. You might even build a loft space to get your beds off the ground. This creates tons of space on the floor for a study table, couch, chair, or little refrigerator. Check with the college about what you can and can't do, but I highly suggest getting the dimensions and building a loft. And when you're decorating, don't forget the family pictures.

Obey the rules. As you live in this little community called a dorm, there will be some rules to live by. It's important that you obey the rules even if you don't think they're important. The dorm and the college have been around longer than you have, so there are probably good reasons for these rules. They'll range from quiet hours to which appliances you can and can't have in your room. There are probably things you'd love to bring because you can't live without them, but not everyone wants to smell pine-scented candles burning down the hallway when it isn't Christmastime. Dorm life might be a great character-development area for God to use to grow your spiritual life. Just live within the rules.

Meet and get to know your Resident Assistant and Resident Director. This is a very important tip for you. Build a good relationship with these two leaders. They are the "trained professionals" hired to help keep the peace, so it's always good to know them. Dorm life could be a little smoother if you smile and talk to these people. They don't have an easy job, but you could make their jobs easier by offering to help out once in a while.

Taking these tips to heart will help you to have an enjoyable experience with dorm life. And a big part of living in the dorm is your roommate(s), so let's take a moment now to talk about them behind their back(s).

Roommates

Throughout my college experience, I had a few roommates and later housemates (after moving out of the dorm and into a house on campus). My first roommate and I did not see eye to eye about what to store in the refrigerator and who not to let spend the night in our dorm room. My second roommate had a different sexual orientation than what my Christian worldview included. My housemates held to a variety of beliefs and lifestyles, but one in particular was a good friend throughout my college experience. Today, he's working with a prominent Christian mission organization after serving on the mission field for several years. Roommates can be tricky to navigate. Some will work out and some won't. This is a normal part of dorm life.

Living with a roommate or two is good training for real life. It's a testing zone for useful communication, compromise (in minor areas), and conflict resolution. It can be a little disconcerting to think about living in a tiny room with someone you don't know. Many who graduate from high school and head off to college to live with an unknown roommate for the first time have a little fear. This is normal. Nearly everyone who doesn't know their roommate ahead of time has some reservations at first. Remember, your roommate probably feels the same way about you. Here are some thoughts to help you along the way.

Have a conversation about cleanliness. You might have different expectations about what the dorm room will look like in three weeks. If neither of you care about that, then press on; but if you do care, it's worth communicating. Be honest about your personal housekeeping habits.

Don't share everything. It might seem like a great idea to share the TV, hairdryer, shampoo, popcorn, and fork; but you'll soon begin to discover that bad things happen. You don't need to feel guilty about having boundaries about your stuff. If you're a Christian, you need to be loving and kind, but sharing everything isn't required. Think ahead of time about the kinds of things you feel comfortable sharing. Prior to arriving on campus, have a conversation on the phone about this area.

Make strides to become friends with your roommate. You might find that you were meant to be together and will become best friends. Lots of great things can happen if you get to know each other. At the very least, friendly overtures will help the time you live together run smoothly, for however long or short that is.

Pray for your roommate. Even before you arrive on campus, pray for your roommate's experience in college and for your relationship with him or her.

Arrange time to be alone. Maybe you could even develop a secret code related to privacy in the dorm room. It could be something hung on the doorknob or a time of day you agree upon. Sometimes you or your roommate will need a little peace and quiet that you can count on.

Take the time to communicate your expectations and have a blast getting to know someone new. When conflict arises, it's always easier to handle when you know the person. With God's help, this roommate has the potential to be a lifelong friend.

QUESTIONS FOR THE JOURNEY

1. What element of dorm life are you most looking forward to? What experience have you already had?

2. What are you excited about with your roommate, and what are your reservations? Why?

3. How can you make the most of your dorm life experience over the next few years?

4. What will you do in the first few weeks to help build relationships and connect with the activities in the dorm?

CHAPTER 18

Campus:
Getting Connected
and Involved

*I was pretty good at debating in high school, so I used that as a way
for me to get involved in college too.*

—Joe, 24

*The true object of all human life is play. Earth is a task garden;
heaven is a playground.*

—G. K. Chesterton

Beyond an Education

The primary reason you're heading off to college is to get a great education for the glory of God. But college goes beyond the classroom. No matter where you enroll, the opportunities to get involved are endless. This experience will give you a million chances to glorify God as you learn about life, people, and yourself while growing into a mature Jesus-following adult.

Those first few weeks on my college campus were difficult. I was a Christian and an athlete, so the first place I looked for connecting points with friends and faith was a Christian organization called Fellowship of Christian Athletes. It was a fantastic place to meet new students, learn about the Bible, and grow in my leadership skills as I quickly jumped into servant-leadership roles. I was also an elementary education student, so as those first few years passed there were opportunities to get to know other future teachers on campus. Classes and clubs offered many opportunities to get to know lifelong friends with a likeminded worldview.

As soon as you arrive on campus, get involved. Sitting in your room by yourself encourages homesickness (and that will happen on its own). It's a little nerve-racking and uncomfortable, but you'll eventually get over the hump of awkwardness. Involvement gives you a voice on campus and confidence with your surroundings. You will learn about your personal strengths and weaknesses. You will learn your God-given skills and get experience. It will also give you many opportunities to develop new interests.

Places to Connect on Campus

Books could be written about the number of places to connect on the college campus. We'll only skim the surface in this section, but I want to give you a broad menu of places to look so you don't miss them. There are lots of groups, societies, and clubs to research. Most universities have a "student life" section on their webpage that's very helpful in providing all the information and contacts for these places. Check them out and give the leaders a call before you land on campus. Once you arrive, take them out for coffee and ask questions. Here are several such places:

> Faith- or religion-based clubs, such as Campus Crusade, InterVarsity, Navigators, Fellowship of Christian Athletes, and others (or, unfortunately, anti-religious groups like the atheists)

Political groups are a great place to make your voice heard, and you can debate the death penalty and abortion issues.

Talent and hobby groups let you connect with others who have similar interests, anything from scrapbooking to playing an instrument.

Educational groups help students study a foreign language, do science projects, or work out math equations.

Lifestyle groups celebrate everything from eating habits, like being a vegetarian, to sexual orientation.

Social justice groups allow you to raise awareness about AIDS in Africa, famine in Somalia, and poverty in Haiti.

The arts and theater programs are a part of nearly every campus. Many who are involved in acting club have theater majors, but not all.

There could be local-interest clubs based on geography. For instance, in Colorado, there are hiking groups. In California, surfing clubs are big.

Culture groups take an interest in wine, art, and music.

Sports are always a big part of campus life, and intramural sports can be a great way to connect without having to be a professional athlete.

Student government goes beyond political clubs. Maybe you weren't the school president in high school, but perhaps you'd like to run for office and make a difference on your campus.

Many sororities and fraternities exist on college and university campuses. Some are Christian based and others are business based. Do your research before joining one. Find out the organization's history, beliefs, focus, moral standing, and reputation in that area. These can be great connecting points for new students, or they can send you down a difficult path as a Christian. Be wise and discerning before you jump in.

Save Time to Volunteer

Your life on campus will be full. If you get connected with even just one of these opportunities in addition to your studies, then your calendar will be overflowing. But it's always good to give of your time for free. Make an effort to volunteer a few hours each month (at least). Maybe it's with your local church. Maybe it's on campus. Take a look in your heart to determine where you should volunteer. Is it with children or teenagers? Do you love using your hands to build things?

There are many places to volunteer, and I'd look to your local church first. In chapter 21, I share about the importance of connecting to a local church while you're in college. But for now, just look at the options there. Outside the church, there are more than 600,000 charities and nonprofit organizations longing for more volunteers. Here are just a few: World Vision, Big Brothers Big Sisters, the Salvation Army, Girl Scouts or Boy Scouts, Habitat for Humanity, YMCA, Boys and Girls Club, the Red Cross, and homeless shelters or other parachurch ministries in your college town. Do a little research and ask some questions, but be sure to volunteer.

When you volunteer, you're living out Jesus's command to be light in the community. You aren't getting a financial reward, but a heart reward. The chance to see and experience someone else's reality will impact you. Volunteering takes the focus off of you and puts it on someone else while you're living out the love-one-another commandment of the Bible. It can't hurt your résumé either.

Don't Forget to Rest

Campus life is full of growing experiences. Get involved and have fun connecting with different people as you live out your faith in Jesus. But let me wrap up this chapter with a warning. This might seem like a weird thing to say after telling you how important it is to get involved, volunteer, and fellowship with friends, but sometimes you need to take a break. Pace yourself. Get off campus by yourself for rest and relaxation. I love coffee shops for this very reason. Some like to use them to connect with people, and I do plenty of that too. But other times, just heading there by yourself is refreshing.

Don't volunteer or connect with people and be involved in twenty different groups every week. God created the world in six days for a reason. On the seventh day, he rested from his great work. This is a model for you during these important years. Set the rhythm for rest before you land on campus. Yes, get involved, but don't overdo it. Take a day once a week to rest and make time for yourself. It will pay off in the real world too.

Years ago when my ministry focused on college students, I organized a college ministry retreat with our local church. I called it the "Sabbath Retreat." Do you know where I'm going with this? We purposely gave twentysomethings time to unwind, take a break, and rest. I gave them some tools to study the Bible and pray, but I also suggested they take a nap, go for a run, sit in the sun, read a book, hike in the woods, or do nothing. Every one of them loved the retreat. It was nice to just relax and rest. Don't wait for someone to organize a retreat for you. Set your own half-day, full-day, or weekend retreats throughout the year. You'll be glad you did.

Enjoy this tremendous opportunity to get connected and involved in the life of your college campus, but also take time to volunteer and rest. You are setting rhythms for the rest of your life.

Questions for the Journey

1. What are your greatest interests? Could they overlap with opportunities on your college campus? Where?

2. How will you use some time to volunteer in your community?

3. How will you build boundaries into your life so you don't burn out but get the kind of healthy rest you need? Where and when will you take this time?

CHAPTER 19

Mentoring: Spiritual Growth with Others

I want to find a mentor who knows Christ and Scripture, who has wisdom, and who is trustworthy.

—Annabel, 15

Go and make disciples.

—Jesus, Matthew 28:19

The Need for Mentors

Everywhere I go to speak and teach, I hear high school students and young adults asking, "Where is the older generation of Christians who should be pouring their lives into us? Where are the folks who can model what it means to be a mature adult follower of Christ?" These people are out there. Instead of wondering why they haven't found you, go and find them! It's your responsibility to seek out the wisdom of those who've traveled the road of faith before you.

Let's call these people who are just a little further along in their journeys with Jesus *mentors*. They come in all shapes and sizes. The reason you pursue a mentor is because you see something in them that you want to imitate. Maybe it's the way they approach career, family, or ministry. Perhaps their integrity, character, or skills are attractive. As they imitate the words and actions of Jesus, you want to imitate their words and actions.

Paul invited the church to follow his example even as he followed the example of Christ (1 Corinthians 4:16; 1 Thessalonians 1:6). We should do the same in our own efforts to follow Jesus, looking not only to Paul, but also to the mentors we find around us.

What Mentors Are — and Aren't

All of us need someone in our lives who's spiritually running ahead of us, who's been following Jesus a little longer. We need role models who can help us evaluate our feelings, thoughts, habits, motives, schedules, and goals.

This might sound scary or intimidating. You might be thinking, *Are you asking me to share my whole life with someone?* Maybe — that all depends on the relationship you establish with your mentor. Ideally, there's a transparency and depth to the relationship that allows you both to share the triumphs and struggles of your lives.

Before we think any further about finding a mentor, let me tell you what you're *not* looking for in a potential mentor. Mentors aren't perfect. They make mistakes, so don't be disillusioned when they fail. Mentors aren't there to help you gain fame and fortune. And they aren't superheroes: The person you're looking for isn't Superman or Wonder Woman. A good mentor is human like you, but just a little further along in his or her spiritual maturity and life experience.

I like the way my friend Eddie, who's in his twenties, described what he's looking for in a mentor:

A good mentor is someone with more life experience than me, someone my

> *A mentor is someone who loves God with all their heart, has their head on straight, and knows what they're looking for. They don't settle and don't give up.*
>
> — Candice, 17

same gender, someone who is more spiritually mature than me, someone who has a desire to see me grow and become more mature than I am. A mentor is someone I trust my life with, a person I know I can get good advice from.

> *A good mentor is someone who has a relationship with God that has developed through the years and has a heart for sharing the lessons they have learned along the way.*
>
> —Ryan, 24

Mentors are mature friends, more like a beloved aunt or uncle than a strict father or mother. A good mentor will celebrate your strengths and allow you to share your weaknesses without condemnation. Mentors are rare individuals who can weep with us, teach us, correct us when necessary, love us deeply, see our greatest potential, and never give up on us. This is the type of person you need in your life.

Here are a few more characteristics I would look for in a mentor:

Look for a *servant*. Good mentors are able to give of themselves because they understand that Jesus came to serve. This might mean they give of their wisdom, resources, and time.

Look for someone who's *loyal*. You need someone who sees a commitment to you as part of his or her life and ministry. Talk about this with the person and ask, "How important is this relationship to you?" You need a mentor to be trustworthy and reliable.

Look for a mentor who's *authentic*. In a world full of fake people on stages and movie screens, you need a mentor who's real—someone who's as genuine as they seem. You don't want someone who's one kind of person "on stage" but another kind when the spotlights aren't on them. You want someone who'll be open with you, admit their mistakes, get excited about your successes, and show a transparent genuineness.

Look for someone who's *honest*. You need a mentor who will look at you objectively and willingly speak truth about your weaknesses and strengths. As you grow into a spiritually mature adult, you need honest and open mentors around you. (And when they tell you the truth, you shouldn't get defensive—you need to remain teachable.)

To sum it up, the best mentors are people who pursue God with everything they have and want to help others do so too. Look for their godly character. Watch how they treat people with their words and actions. Don't look for perfection but brokenness and humility. They should remind you of Jesus.

> *A good mentor is someone who is, for the most part, spiritually sound. He or she needs to be someone you can trust and who is willing to listen to you and give you good, Christian advice.*
>
> —Jaclyn, 17

Finding a Mentor

So now you know some of the characteristics you're looking for in a mentor, but how do you find one? Here are some suggestions:

Pray for God's wisdom. Spend time daily asking the Lord to bring to your mind and heart the right person for the right area of your life. Then open your eyes and ears and see what God does.

Keep your expectations realistic. Many who make this transition into the real world have a perfect person in mind who'll be their mentoring "savior." But they are sure to be disappointed. The Messiah has already come, and his name is Jesus. You're not looking for someone who's perfect. Look for a real human being who can share in your life.

> *My mentor is a woman whom I totally respect. She's happy with whatever Jesus provides and looks to him for answers to her questions. She is in step with God. I want to follow her.*
>
> —Haylee, 15

Stay alert to potential mentors. Your mentor might be someone who lives in your neighborhood or attends your church—or he or she might be someone who doesn't have these natural connections. If the person lives far away, you might need to travel to find this person and meet only occasionally, staying in contact mainly through emails and phone calls. You never know: Your mentor might be a college professor. I had plenty of college professors who served as my mentors. It was partly through their deep-rooted impact in my life that God has orchestrated the writing of this book. There are many spiritually mature Jesus-followers who could serve as your mentor. You just need to keep your eyes and ears open, and you'll find them.

> *If you're a young girl, you should find an older woman who is strong in her faith in Jesus. Spend time with her. Listen to her wisdom: It can be so helpful for your whole life.*
>
> —Gloria, 18

Keep in mind that you may want to have more than one mentor. As different seasons come and go, as you further discover the person God is helping you to become, you might need a disciple who's modeling Christ in front of you, an advocate who's fighting for justice in the world, or an artist who's emulating creativity. You might also want to look for a mentor of your own gender, as that can make talking about certain issues much easier. Your mentors will change over time, so your antenna should always be up. Keep looking for those who will invest in you face to face, but also understand that some may mentor you through books, magazine articles, sermons, or songs. Assemble a collection of mentors to help you negotiate your strategic transition into the real world.

Becoming a Mentor

Now let me turn the tables. When you choose to customize and take control of your life the way God intended, excitement will begin boiling in your blood. The new freedom of the real world brings with it new freedom with your time. As you begin to pray and study Scripture more, your life will be filled to the brim. Like a dam that sprouts one little hole, then two, then eight, then forty, then—BANG!—it breaks wide open, you'll begin overflowing with love for God and others. Where does all the overflow go?

It's God's design for you to invest this extra into someone else. You need to share the overflow of your love and intimacy with God. As your faith matures, you need to mentor others.

So where can you find someone to mentor? Well, look at your life. Where do you hang out? Maybe there's someone at your school or workplace. Maybe there's someone at your church or campus ministry. Keep your eyes and ears open for someone who might benefit from you humbly coming alongside of them. Don't force it. Let it happen naturally by God's divine direction.

Pray that God would show you someone in whom you might be able to invest your life. Remember that mentoring is a humble endeavor. Offering to walk alongside someone, to help that person grow in faith, is delicate work. Pray for God to orchestrate a divine appointment for you. As you're praying, begin looking for the right person to mentor. Here's a quick list of questions to ask yourself when you think you've spotted someone you might mentor:

Is this person *teachable?* This person needs a heart that's willing to learn. Just as the disciples followed Jesus as students, this person will be following you (maybe with their notebook in hand), ready to learn how to live for Jesus better. Is her heart open to God? Do you sense any pride? These could be stumbling blocks in the mentoring relationship or teachable moments.

Will this person take *initiative?* Does he crave spiritual milk or solid food? He must be willing to take the steps necessary to have a mentoring relationship with you. It can't be like pulling teeth.

Is this person *hungry?* The person you mentor must have a passion to grow and become all God wants her to be. Is there a spirit about her that hungers and thirsts for God?

Is this person *faithful?* Will this person keep his commitments? Will he show up on time to your meetings and outings? Faithfulness to God is first; faithfulness to you is next. The person you mentor must be willing to commit.

Is this person *available?* This person needs to be able to devote time to the mentoring relationship. Is her schedule too full to work this in? Is she willing to drop some things that are not as important for the sake of this relationship with you? This person must make herself available for growth opportunities if this is going to work.

Is this person *trustworthy*? You want to mentor someone whose character is as deep as his gifts and abilities. He doesn't have to be the "star of the show," just trustworthy. If the person isn't responsible, it won't work. In addition, will this person follow through on an assignment you give him? He needs the ability to receive instructions and make things happen. Is he reliable?

Remember, you're not looking for someone who's perfect. You're just looking for someone who's eager to grow in faith. This person probably looks up to you as a model of Jesus, but is she willing to follow after you as you follow Christ?

A Model for Mentoring

There are so many mentoring relationships throughout history, starting with those in Scripture. Can you think of any? Tim Elmore explores thirty-two of these relationships in his book, *The Greatest Mentors in the Bible* (Kingdom, 1996). Here are a few examples: Abraham and Lot, Naomi and Ruth, Jonathan and David, Elizabeth and Mary, Barnabas and Paul, and, of course, Jesus and his disciples.

Did you realize there were so many of these relationships throughout Scripture? Check out Elmore's book sometime. Look up the names, read over the stories, and think about the impact these mentors had on their mentees.

Let's take a deeper look at one of these relationships—the relationship between two cousins, Elizabeth (the mother of John the Baptist) and Mary (the mother of Jesus). The gospel of Luke begins with the story of Elizabeth, an older woman who had no children. One day an angel told Liz's husband, Zechariah, that Elizabeth would become pregnant and give birth to a son who would become a messenger of God's good news.

But in the sixth month of that surprising pregnancy, Liz's young cousin Mary received some even more unbelievable news from the angel Gabriel: She, though a virgin, would become pregnant and give birth to the Messiah. No big deal, right? Wrong! This angelic meeting changed Mary's life and the course of history. This kind of news would cause the average person to go into shock and end up in the hospital. *Call 911. Mary's just fainted.*

So what does this young Jewish girl do? She immediately finds someone to tell. (You would too, wouldn't you?) She went to Liz. Apparently Mary thought highly of her. I think Mary knew she was a great lover of people. I can imagine Elizabeth listening on the edge of her seat and asking questions as Mary relayed her encounter with Gabriel: *What happened next? How big was Gabriel? Did he have wings? Were you scared? Tell me more! What else did he say? What did you say next?* I think there would have been great excitement in Liz's voice as Mary shared this history-shaking news.

Liz is a great example of a mentor who invested in another person's life. (You can read the whole story for yourself in Luke 1:5–56.) These two women were available to one another and ready to listen. We all need people in our lives who will engage with us as we share big news and big events. Let your cup overflow from passion and find someone to share your story with as you follow Jesus into college and beyond.

QUESTIONS FOR THE JOURNEY

1. Have you ever had a mentor or been a mentor to someone? Describe the experience.

2. What are the benefits of having others in your life who are a little further along in their relationship with Jesus?

3. When you have questions about Jesus, the Bible, or the church, to whom do you bring these questions?

4. What steps can you take to find a mentor and be a mentor as you make this transition out of high school?

CHAPTER 20

Dating and Sex: Searching for a Spouse

I plan to find someone who loves me for who I truly am and is a godly person. I believe God has the perfect person in store for me in my future.

—Laura, 17

Blessed are the pure in heart, for they will see God.

—Jesus, Matthew 5:8

Cloud Nine

I still remember the moment I spotted her in the airport. She was sitting on the terminal floor writing creative notes. Her sandy blonde hair was full of curls. When she looked up at me, her beautiful bluish-green eyes (with a hint of yellow) melted my heart. I tried to talk to her but stumbled over my words. She was flying to the same place I was. Our two teams of college students had merged to cross the ocean on a short-term mission experience to Romania.

The second memory I have of her was in the middle of our time in Romania. We were on a bus heading to a ministry service location. Her black sunglasses covered her stunning eyes. I was captured by her beauty and intrigued by her mystery. Sparks were flying in my heart, but we were on a mission trip and serving Jesus. All else would have to wait until we returned home. It did.

> *I intend to look for a woman whom I can trust, whom I can respect, whom I can love, and with whom I can imagine sharing my life.*
>
> —Tom, 16

When we got back to the States, Laurie and I started dating. I'll admit I was caught off guard—first by her looks, and then by her heart for Jesus. The more we talked, the closer we became. Month by month, our relationship deepened. Eventually we got engaged and then married. We've been growing in our relationship with each other for seventeen years and counting.

If you'd told me during our first month of dating that I'd love her more seventeen years later than I did at the time, I would have said, "No way! I could never love her more than I do now. This is as good as it gets." But I would've been so wrong. My love for Laurie is miles wider and deeper today. Why? I know her so much better today than I did fourteen years ago.

Do you have your own story about falling in love? Are you still hoping to meet that special someone, or are you planning to stay single? If you've dated, have your experiences been healthy or harmful?

With the right principles in place, finding the right person, dating, and marrying can be one of the most exciting journeys you'll ever take. But before we talk anymore about that possibility, let's start with being single.

A Word or Two on the Single Life

Is it possible that being single is better than being married?

We all start out single. If you're reading this as you're preparing to leave high school, you're most likely single. Maybe you assume you'll find a special someone someday. Or maybe not. But let's think a little bit about the single life.

Being single is a great thing. It's not second-class status to being married, and it's not just a transitional stage. Many people in the Bible found they were able to more fully devote their lives to God as singles. The apostle Paul took full advantage of his singleness: He traveled the world, shared the gospel of Jesus, planted churches, and found time to write most of the New Testament. Would he have

> *I want to find a man who's running as fast as he can toward God. I know that God holds my future in his hands, and that's all I need to know.*
>
> — Brooke, 17

been able to do that if he'd had a wife and five kids? Maybe—but he definitely took advantage of his singleness.

If you're single, celebrate your singleness. Take advantage of the benefits because singleness is an honorable calling. Many throughout history have used their singleness to advance the kingdom— including Jesus!

There will be moments when your soul is yelling, *This is great! I have so much freedom! I'm so content!* But there might be times when you feel lonely and find yourself wishing you had another person to share your life with. In those times remember that Jesus is all you need. I know that might sound like a slogan or a bumper sticker, but it really is true. He's your closest companion, and he longs for you to draw close to him.

Pursuing the Biblical Way

If you're interested in marrying one day, you might wonder if the Bible has any advice on finding your one true love. In fact, there are all kinds of different stories about how people in the Bible made the connection with that special someone. Perhaps you'll want to follow these examples, but probably not.

Guys, you might want to find an attractive female prisoner of war, bring her home, shave her head, trim her nails, and give her new clothes. No kidding. This was God's idea for the Israelites back in the day (Deuteronomy 21:11–13).Or you might try marrying a prostitute to help people understand God's faithfulness. That's what Hosea did when he was told to marry Gomer (Hosea 1:1–3).

> *A healthy dating relationship looks like a marathon, not a sprint. Both people are mature enough to know that they'll have as long as they want to get to know each other, so they don't have to do anything impure to keep the other's attention. It's a friendship.*
>
> —Shae, 18

Ladies, you might watch out for a man seeking to impress you by defending your right to take well water for your flock of sheep. That's how Moses captured the heart of his wife (Exodus 2:16–21).

Guys, you could agree to work seven years in exchange for a woman's hand in marriage. But be careful: You might get tricked into marrying the wrong woman and then have to work another seven years for the woman you wanted in the first place. That's what happened to Jacob (Genesis 29:15–30).Or you could find a spouse by going to a party, grabbing a woman, and carrying her off to be your wife. This was the Benjamites' plan for marriage (Judges 21:9–25).

If you prefer the gross way of winning love, try killing two hundred men in battle, cutting off their foreskins, and presenting them to your future father-in-law in exchange for his daughter's hand. That's what David did (1 Samuel 18:27).

Need more ideas? How about these:

You could become the emperor of a huge nation and hold a beauty contest. That's what Xerxes did to win the heart of Esther. Well, sort of (Esther 2:3–4).

Still desperate for a date? Maybe your parents could help. Next time you see someone you like, go home and tell your parents, "I have seen a woman I like. Now get her for me." This might have been Samson's first mistake (Judges 14:1–3).

Maybe you're being too picky. Make up for quality with quantity. Solomon had a bunch of wives (1 Kings 11:1–3).

If worst comes to worst, beg God to create a wife for you while you're sleeping. But be careful; it'll cost you a rib. This was Adam's story (Genesis 2:19–24).

Yes, it's true — every single one of those examples is in the Bible. But relax: I'm not suggesting you try any of them. Times have changed a little bit. Okay, times have changed a lot. Some of these examples had a great deal to do with the culture of the day, where a wife was considered to be more a man's property than his partner. And it's important to remember that not all of these examples were God's idea. With marriage (as in other areas), sometimes the people of the Bible took things into their own hands while ignoring God's best commands for their lives.

> *Become close friends first, then take the step to start dating. Don't put yourself in a tempting position. Share your boundaries and expectations. TAKE IT SLOW!*
>
> — Stephanie, 18

So let's get a little more serious now. As you head out of high school, you might have had some dating experiences, or maybe not. Either way, it's critical that you lay down some relationship boundaries as you seek to become a mature, Christ-following adult.

The Goal of Dating

So what's the purpose of dating? Think about it. Why are you looking for a date? Is it to find a spouse? Is it to fulfill your sex drive? To cure your loneliness? To have a fairy-tale romance? Is there another reason?

From the beginning God understood it wasn't good for Adam to be alone (Genesis 1–2). Plants and animals didn't fulfill the human need for authentic friendship, companionship, and love that another human being could supply. Enter Eve, stage right! She really was Miss Right. I can imagine Adam groggily waking up from his surgery, now minus a rib. He must've rubbed his eyes, yawned, laid eyes on Eve, and then jumped to his feet and said, "Whoa, man!" (wo-man .... get it? Just keep reading.)

Both men and women were made in God's image. Or, to say it another way, the image of God is fully represented by the completeness of man and woman together. Men and women are different, have you noticed? Not just physically, but in many areas and desires. They bring different qualities to relationships, but together they make up the image of God. To see the complete view of God, we must take a view of the "oneness" of woman and man. Together there is completeness, wholeness, safety, security, and love.

The difficulties for Adam and Eve start when selfishness, brokenness, and loneliness enter the world because of their choice to be like God and eat from the forbidden tree in the garden. Pride caused them to realize they were naked. The true nature of the relationship was broken. If you're in a relationship and tension, miscommunication, unmet expectations, and arguments arise, blame it on Adam and Eve. Really, they started this mess. As a result, we too must take ownership of our own mistakes against God.

Your goal in dating should be to find the Adam to your Eve. (Or find the Eve to your Adam.) It's as Sid the sloth, eyes aflutter, said with humor to Diego the saber-toothed tiger in the movie *Ice Age*: "You complete me!" We need people in our lives to make a loving connection. This love comes from friendships of all levels — but for some of us, it's found most profoundly in loving a partner for life.

True Love

Before we got married, Laurie and I decided to have a Scripture reference engraved inside our wedding rings. The engravings read 1 COR. 13:4–8. It's a passage from one of Paul's letters to a church in Corinth, and he talks about love. These verses are often read at weddings — but the love they describe is greater than romantic love. You can use these verses as guidelines for what it means to be loving not only in a dating relationship with someone you might marry, but in all of your relationships:

> Love is patient, love is kind. It does not envy, it does not boast, it is not proud. It does not dishonor others, it is not self-seeking, it is not easily angered, it keeps no record of wrongs. Love does not delight in evil but

rejoices with the truth. It always protects, always trusts, always hopes, always perseveres. Love never fails.

As you seek to become a more loving person, you may find that some elements of the verses above will come naturally to you. Others will be a struggle. It'll become a daily choice to be patient or kind when your first impulse is to be quick-tempered or cruel. When someone you love hurts you, it's difficult to forget. Still, you'll need to let go of the hurt and embrace love. It's a choice we must make over and over not only in dating and marriage, but in all aspects of life. But let me go through these verses and comment on how I see them particularly reflected in dating and marriage.

Love is patient—even in trying circumstances. I'm very patient when things are going my way, aren't you? It's easy when things are moving along as planned. But when they aren't, that's the real test of patience. Don't be impatient. Don't rush ahead in your relationship. I know, "He's soooooo good-looking," and "She's hot!" Use your brain more than your heart. It'll save you hurt and bring health to your relationship down the road.

Love is kind when faced with unkindness. It's so easy to hurt one another and so easy to forget to do those little kind deeds. Love chooses to be kind regardless of the response because love is committed to giving, not receiving. The person you love might be difficult at times, but love chooses to serve no matter what.

Love is never jealous or vain. You shouldn't worry about who he's with when he's not with you. If you have jealously issues, you're not expressing love. Talk about it. Clear it up. Love isn't jealous.

Love gives when it feels more natural to be selfish and hold on. It's a challenge you'll face throughout your life. Suppose you've finally finished your physics paper and you're ready to relax. You look over

> *I want to find a woman whom I care for deeply and get to know for as long as it takes until I'm sure I want to spend the rest of my life with her. I'll stay content, telling myself it's worth the wait.*
>
> *—Bradley, 16*

and see that your loved one is still struggling to write their paper. Do you offer to help or pretend you didn't notice? Love gets up and keeps going. Love gives a little more.

Love keeps no record of wrongs. Love chooses to forgive and forget. Has someone you love wronged you? Chances are good that you've been hurt already. Don't let this slow you down from trusting and loving one another. Do all you can to move into the future with freedom.

Love takes joy in being fully truthful because the truth sets you free. Don't hide anything from the one you love. Share it tactfully, carefully, and in the right timing. Always live in truth, and you will find peace.

Love believes, trusts, hopes, and keeps on keeping on. If no one else believes in you, make sure you believe in the one you love. Love never fails.

You can be sure there will be stretching times when your faith in God and your love will be tested. You'll be at your limit sometimes and wonder how you can keep going. You can! Love will keep you going. Love from God is your anchor in the storm. In those stretching times, may you find yourselves holding hands in love, and may you find this to be enough.

The Physical Side

It's natural for two people in love to feel physically attracted to each other. But our physical drive can too easily become a desire for quick, selfish gratification and pleasure. The flipside of love is selfishness, and lust is driven by selfishness. Test your actions against 1 Corinthians 13. If you're putting the other person's needs before your own, you're most likely pursuing the relationship in a truly loving manner. But if you're just in the relationship to get something for yourself, you can be sure it's not love. Test your motives. Are you dying to self or just dying for a date?

As people pursue love, they often face a question regarding

their physical relationship: "How far is too far?" Some people will say, "Well, as long as we don't have *sexual intercourse*, we're okay — right?" I think these questions

> *More communication.*
> *Less touching.*
> — Brooke, 17

really have to do with the relationship between commitment and sexual activity.

The longer a couple is together, the more commitment typically exists in the relationship. This isn't always the case, but most of the time if a couple has been together for a long time, there's a higher commitment level. Sometimes couples are together way too long. They know the relationship isn't headed toward a lifelong commitment in marriage, but they refuse to cut if off for whatever reason (possibly because they're too far along emotionally and physically). Other times they're just "friends with benefits," taking advantage of each other physically. They think they can handle it, but they're actually hurting themselves and their partner both emotionally and spiritually.

In a healthy relationship, the level of physical activity won't exceed the level of commitment. Healthy relationships move along slowly and deliberately. Take a look at the chart below:

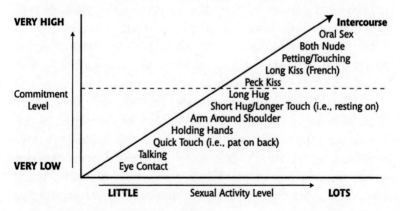

In my estimation the biggest obstacle to obtaining a healthy, loving dating relationship with another person is the tension between the horizontal and vertical lines. The problem occurs when the commitment and amount of time the couple has spent together is low, but the level of sexual activity is high.

The next question many dating couples ask is, "But how much time needs to pass before we can [fill in the blank]?" Here's my suggestion: Don't worry about moving up the arrow to the right. It will happen on its own as time passes, conversations are had, the commitment level grows, and trust is built. This can take months, even years, and that's a good thing. Take a look at the dotted line. When you pass the dotted line, it's easy to reach a point of no return where your will power isn't strong enough to resist sexual tempta- tion. That's why certain levels of sexual activity belong only within the lifelong commitment of a marriage. I'd suggest you avoid going beyond the dotted line until you've entered marriage with a lifelong partner. Remember 1 Corinthians 13? The key is to stay focused on your relationship with Jesus and allow God to direct you as a couple.

Suppose Jimmy and Pam hook up at a party and have sexual intercourse. They spent two hours together and have no real com- mitment to each other, but they engaged in acts God wants us to save for marriage. Sexual intercourse, as well as many of the physi- cal acts leading to sexual intercourse, is reserved for marriage only. The emotional, spiritual, and sometimes physical damage that can occur from engaging in these activities outside the commitment of marriage are devastating. And you know what's tragic? Night after night, more and more lives are ravaged by sexual sin.

I believe most of us intuitively understand this. Of a survey of three thousand women, 80 percent said they regretted having casual sex before marriage.[1] We know before it happens that it's not God's best for us; it's not healthy. This kind of living damages future relationships and slows down your hope of finding Mr. or Mrs. Right. Every time you decide to engage in temporary pleasure

[1] Alexa Joy Sherman and Nicole Tocantins, *The Happy Hook-Up: A Single Girl's Guide to Casual Sex* (Berkeley, CA: Ten Speed Press, 2004), 26.

with someone you're not married to, you damage yourself and the health of your future relationships.

Here's another scenario: Ed and Sally have dated for four months. During the course of their relationship, the physical side of things has moved from holding hands and hugging to kissing and petting—and last night they had sexual intercourse for the first time. Their self-control weakened over the months until it disappeared altogether. Their desire for one another (lust) became a driving force in their relationship. Love for God and love for one another is no longer driving their relationship.

Ed and Sally are both followers of Jesus, but they're struggling spiritually in their relationships with God and each other. They think they're in love; but according to God's best for their lives, their actions are selfish. They finally break off their relationship, and it's emotionally damaging to both. Each day, this scenario happens over and over again in the real world.

What If I've Already Crossed the Line?

If your physical relationship with someone has already gone further than it should have, seek God. Ask him to forgive you. Ask the person you had relations with to forgive you. Admit your selfishness.

Here's the good news: Regardless of what's happened in the past—whether it was last night or last year—God longs to have a close relationship with you. He wants your heart right now, whether you're returning to him again or coming to him for the very first time. No matter what your mistakes have been, there's nothing so bad that he won't forgive you. (See Mark 3:28.)

You can always have a fresh start at building a healthy, God-honoring relationship. Jesus won't hold your mistakes against you in the future, but he does want you to change your way of thinking so you won't continue to make the same mistakes as you grow into a mature, Jesus-following adult. Be encouraged: His compassion is new every morning (Lamentations 3:22–24).

After asking God for forgiveness, set boundaries—today! Look at the chart and ask yourself how far you'll move in future relationships as you seek to truly love your dating partner.

Keeping Love Alive

As you enter a relationship and pursue love with someone else, commit yourself to serving that person. Look for ways to fan the flames of love. Go on a picnic, take a walk together, watch a movie with a group, find something to laugh about, or write each other encouraging notes. As you head through the steps of dating toward engagement and marriage, never let romance wane. It takes effort to be romantic, but it's worth it. Romance isn't just about sexual attraction; it involves the whole being of a person. Having a great conversation can be romantic.

When you're angry, deal with it. Do your best to get rid of anger before the day is over. Never talk *at* one another; this isn't loving. Never speak loudly at one another unless the house (or apartment or dorm room or Starbucks) is on fire. Don't try to find fault with one another; give the benefit of the doubt. If there's a disagreement, remember the goal isn't to win the argument but to love one another in the process.

Never leave one another without a warm word (and a loving embrace, if you've been dating a while). As you build trust with this person, begin to save the very best events of your day for the one you love. It's always the most fun the first time you share it. Always keep Jesus first in your individual lives, and you'll be amazed at how your dating and marriage relationship flourishes.

Most of all, keep God at the center of your relationship. Maybe you've seen the following triangle diagram. God is at the top; you and the person who "caught your eye" are on opposite sides of the base.

As each of you seeks to grow closer to God you'll grow closer to one another. The more intimate you are in your relationship with the One who is Love, the more in love you'll become with each other. Get closer to God through studying the Bible and talking to him all

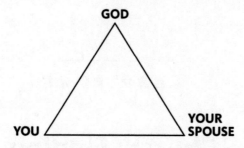

the time. When two people in love each pursue God individually, it's amazing how unstoppable they become together for bringing the kingdom of God to earth. I've known many couples who individually loved Jesus and had an amazing impact on the world together. This kind of relationship isn't always easy, but it is loving.

As you head from high school to life after high school, make peace with the past and move into the future, striving to work primarily on your personal relationship with Jesus. If God brings a special someone into your life, take it slow, lovingly moving forward in the relationship. Keep in mind that healthy dating leads to a healthy marriage, and the marriage is more important than the wedding.

QUESTIONS FOR THE JOURNEY

1. What does healthy dating look like?
2. From this day forward, how can you make sure you don't cross any lines in your relationships with others?
3. Do you see your body as something holy or sacred? What difference does it make to see your body as sacred versus something to be used and destroyed?
4. What qualities do you think are most important in a Christian marriage?

CHAPTER 21

Church: Finding and Investing in a Local Family

A community of believers reminds us we're not alone on this journey. As different and diverse as we may be, we all have something in common that unites us. We can all encourage and support one another as we grow closer to Jesus.

— Ryan, 24

God placed all things under his feet and appointed him to be head over everything for the church, which is his body, the fullness of him who fills everything in every way.

— Ephesians 1:22 – 23

Homesick

The invitation came from a classmate in elementary school. "Jeff, do you want to sleep over at my house?" I was speechless. No one had asked me that before. I didn't want to hurt Tim's feelings, so I said, "Yes, but I have to ask my parents."

Twenty-four hours later, the deal was sealed. That Friday after school I was heading over to Tim's house to spend the night.

I'd never been to Tim's house before. The minute I arrived that Friday, I started comparing his house with mine. It smelled different. It looked different. His parents were different. The furniture was different. The food was different. The TV shows were different. His bedroom was different.

> *The body of believers keeps me accountable in my walk with God and encourages me if I'm down.*
>
> —Stephanie, 18

It all felt very uncomfortable and, well, different. And like a lot of first-time sleepover participants, I soon felt very homesick. I'm not embarrassed to admit I wanted my mommy. As soon as that "different meal" at that "different kitchen table" was over, I called my parents. They came and picked me up and took me to the comfort, safety, and familiarity of my own home.

Have you ever been homesick? I think we all know how hard it can be to feel far from home. We want to be in a place where we're known and where we belong.

For many, church is just that kind of home, a place of safety and belonging. The church isn't a building; it's a group of people. The church is made up of people who long to know and love Jesus with all of their lives. It's a group of people serving one another and the world around them. Throughout history, from the first church to the many expressions of the local church today, God has longed for us to be in community with other believers. Church is our place to belong.

In the book of Acts, we're given a quick outline of what the first church was up to. Luke tells us the believers "devoted themselves to the apostles' teaching and to fellowship, to the breaking of bread and to prayer" (Acts 2:42). In an age of megachurches with entertainment programs and big budgets, it's possible to lose sight of the purpose of the local church.

As you make your way into adulthood, you need to settle into a local body of believers. You might have heard it said that church membership is optional. This might sound nice, but according to God's Word, that's not what God thinks.

Houston, We Have a Problem

A recent study by the Southern Baptist organization Lifeway Research found that 70 percent of eighteen-year-olds who attend church regularly in high school quit going by age twenty-three. The majority of those young adults eventually return to a local church, but oftentimes it's not until they're married and sometimes not until they have children. More than a third of the people who've left the local church (34 percent) still haven't returned by age thirty.[1] Some never return. This is a tragedy.

The good news? Many young people are connecting with vibrant campus ministries and spending time in community with other believers their age. This is important if you're heading off to college. I love campus ministries—I was on leadership in Fellowship of Christian Athletes during all four of my undergraduate years. Campus ministries are very important. Please get connected.

But even if you find and get involved with a great campus ministry, it's still important to get connected with a local church. There are many passages of Scripture that instruct all believers to deeply connect to a local faith community. Interestingly, Scripture refers to the church as the body of Christ. This metaphor is powerful. Without you, the church is missing some parts. Really. The body must have all of its parts to function in proper order. Just as the body can't function properly without an eye, ear, or big toe (you need it for balance), every local community of faith in Jesus needs a complete body to be healthy.

Paul talked about all of this in his letter to the church in Corinth (1 Corinthians

> *Church helps me know I'm not alone. It's not easy when everyone else doesn't believe in what you do; it's kind of frustrating. Having other people makes it less stressful. When I'm struggling, they usually have pretty good advice.*
>
> —Candice, 17

---

[1] *Leadership Journal,* "Why Many Young Adults Quit," *Christianity Today,* October 1, 2007, www.christianitytoday.com/le/2007/004/10.15.html (accessed September 10, 2012).

12:12 – 31). Paul uses a powerful metaphor of the body to communicate how important it is for you to be connected. You have a part to play in the local church. You might be a hand, foot, ear, or nerve. These are used to accomplish God's purposes on earth, to advance the kingdom. No member is more important than another. Just because one guy stands in front of all those people and teaches doesn't make him more important than the guy who works behind the scenes in the kitchen. We're all vital, and we all need to work together. Within the local church, you'll discover the fullness of the person Christ made you to be, who you are, and where you belong.

> *A community of Jesus-followers helps me by keeping me on the right path with God. They help me reach my goals in life without as many distractions along the way.*
> — Jodi, 15

Paul also says that when one member of the body hurts, the whole body is hurt. If you stub your toe, it's hard not to think about your hurting toe. Your whole body hurts. In another way, when one person falls short of using their gifts, abilities, and passions to their fullest potential, everyone suffers. The church needs everyone to serve in the right spot for the fullest impact.

The Hope of the World

Bill Hybels, senior pastor at Willow Creek Community Church in Chicago, Illinois, says the church is the "hope of the world." I think he's right. Yes, Jesus is the ultimate hope of the world, but if we don't unite with Christ as the head of the church, if we don't all come together as believers of Jesus, we won't be living up to all God has for us.

The church should make a difference in its local community and the world. If a church doesn't reach out and touch the needs of those around it, it really isn't being a church. If a local body of believers suddenly got up and left, the surrounding community should feel the loss because this was the group who was caring for the elderly, the hurting, the suffering, the homeless, and the outcast. The body of believers is so important to God's kingdom plan that Jesus declared the gates of hell won't prevail against it (Matthew 16:18).

Local churches come in all shapes and sizes. You might prefer pews or folding chairs. Perhaps you like classic hymns, or maybe you'd rather hear the songs you listen to on Christian radio. Maybe you prefer a church where the

> *The church is your support group, your true friends. They'll stand with you no matter what — help bring you back if you ever fall away. They're your anchor, your life raft, your survival kit; you can't make it through the hostile waters of life without them. They're invaluable.*
>
> *— Shae, 18*

preacher speaks for only fifteen minutes (good luck!), or one where the worship includes visual arts. You might prefer a church that meets on the beach over one with candles and stained-glass windows. No matter what your personal preferences are, find a local church you can commit to. Even if you know you'll be there for only a few years, plug in, connect with people, become a member, take the senior pastor out to lunch, serve in your areas of giftedness, and make a huge kingdom difference. Become part of a community of believers who are serving God with faithfulness — teaching the Scriptures, breaking bread together (including the Lord's Supper), baptizing new believers, praying with and for one another, fellowshipping with joy, exercising authenticity in their relationships, and serving the world for the sake of advancing the kingdom of God (Acts 2:42 – 44).

Jesus is passionate about the church. All four gospels tell the story of Jesus overturning the tables in his Father's house because of the hiked temple costs and hypocritical living. The disciples sat back and watched, probably wondering if Jesus had lost his mind, until they remembered how the psalmist said, "Zeal for your house will consume me" (Psalm 69:9; John 2:17).

As a Jew, Jesus understood the sanctity of the temple as the house of God. Today, those who seek to follow Jesus are the collective temple of God and comprise the church (1 Corinthians 6:19). Jesus has chosen to live not only everywhere, all the time, but he's also chosen to live inside each of his followers (Colossians 1:27). Today the house of God is the body of Christ, taking the great news of Jesus to a desperate world. If you aren't connected with a local body of believers right now, pay attention to that homesickness you're feeling. The local church needs you, and you need the local church.

> *Community brings encouragement, mostly. Additionally, I believe the prayer of many is more powerful than the prayer of one.*
>
> —John, 16

The writer of Hebrews offers us a great final word about the mission of the church: "Let us consider how we might spur one another on toward love and good deeds, not giving up meeting together, as some are in the habit of doing, but encouraging one another—and all the more as you see the Day approaching" (Hebrews 10:24–25).

Questions for the Journey

1. Would you rather follow Jesus with people around you or do it alone?

2. What troubles you about the local church? What gives you the most joy about the local church?

3. How do you see yourself being connected to the body of Christ while using your gifts and abilities?

4. How will you be proactive in getting connected with a local church when you leave high school?

A Final Word (or Two Thousand): The Next Several Days of Keeping Your Faith

I'm extremely excited to get out into the real world and become who God intends me to be, but I know I need to learn how to keep my priorities in line and use self-discipline before I'll be completely ready for it.

—Jaclyn, 17

Even when I am old and gray,
do not forsake me, my God,
till I declare your power to the next generation,
your mighty acts to all who are to come.

—Psalm 71:18

Take It Slow

You've reached the end of the book. If you've read every word so far, I congratulate you. Well done! If you're picking up this book for the first time and you figured you'd skip to the last chapter to see how the story ends—well, that's okay. But you may want to go back and start at the beginning. If you're the kind of reader who jumps around in a book, or if you've been keeping this book on a shelf for a rainy day, that's fine too. Whatever your reading style, I hope you're finding this book an encouragement in your walk with Jesus.

As I think about you heading out the door to serve Jesus, I remember a morning when my daughter was leaving to catch the school bus after a wintry ice storm. She was hurrying down the driveway with her head raised high, taking long, confident strides as if it were a beautiful, sunny summer day. I knew if she continued down the icy sidewalk at that quick pace, or if she started to run to catch the bus, she'd fall, get hurt, and maybe cry. (And miss the bus!) So as any good parent would do, I yelled, "Lillian, slow down and take shorter steps. Watch out for ice!"

That's my simple advice to you as you make this exciting transition from the world of high school to the world of college and beyond. This transition will require firm footing and good timing. There are many pitfalls and slippery slopes to watch out for in a world filled with temptations and ungodly pleasures. If you run into this life too quickly without looking where you're putting your feet, you'll slip and fall—and the pain will be more than that of a bruise. So take it slow, enjoy the journey, and keep your eyes fixed on Jesus, the One who's "the same yesterday and today and forever" (Hebrews 13:8).

From Child to Adult

The goal of this book has been to help you move toward becoming a mature, Jesus-following adult. It's been about creating space for you to transition from being a child who's largely dependent on your parents, to a young adult who takes increasing responsibility for your own direction while understanding that we're all dependent on God.

Throughout this book I've attempted to give you practical advice for your journey of faith. As you move from childlike faith to mature, adult faith, here are some additional areas to think about. Take a look at each line on the chart below and ask yourself, *Is my faith more childish or more mature in this area?*[1]

---

[1] This chart was adapted from Mark DeVries's book *Family-Based Youth Ministry* (InterVarsity, 1994).

Immature, Childish Faith	Mature Adult Faith
Good Christians don't have pain and disappointment.	God uses our pain and disappointments to make us more faithful followers of Christ.
God helps those who help themselves.	God helps those who admit their own helplessness.
God wants to make us happy.	God wants to make us holy, more like Christ in our words and actions.
Faith will always help us explain what God is doing because things always work my way.	Faith helps us stand under God's divine control even when we have no idea what God's doing.
The closer we get to God, the more perfect we become.	The closer we get to God, the more we become aware of our own sinfulness and dependence on someone to save us.
Mature Christians have all the answers.	Mature Christians can honestly wrestle with tough questions because we trust God has the answers.
Good Christians are always strong.	Our strength is admitting our weakness and dependence on God.
We go to a local church because our friends are there, we have great leaders, and we get something out of it.	We go to church because we belong to the body of Christ and long to serve.

So where do you find yourself on this chart? Which set of statements best matches your own beliefs? Wherever you find yourself, keep in mind that faith is a journey; becoming mature in your faith doesn't happen overnight. I hope you'll keep reading and praying through the themes and chapters of this book so you can continue to become the mature, Jesus-following adult God intends you to be.

Your Next Several Days in the Real World

I've heard it said that it takes twenty-two days to develop a new habit or break an old one. This means you have to do something at least twenty-two days in a row before it begins to become part of your everyday routine. So given all we've talked about in this book, the next twenty-two days or so will be critical. Whether you're just out of high school or have been out for a while, immediately begin to develop habits that honor God and break the ones that don't.

Take another look at the three big themes of this book (and legs of the chair): Identity, Choices, and Belonging. Below are the theme-related questions that I attempted to answer throughout the chapters of this book. Can you answer these questions for yourself with conviction?

Leg One—Identity: Who am I? Who am I supposed to be, and what do I know to be true? Can I doubt sometimes?

Leg Two—Choices: Do my decisions matter? How much control over my life do I have? How do I handle the new responsibilities coming my way as an adult? How will I handle college (or my new job)? Is it okay if I'm stressed out?

Leg Three—Belonging: Where do I fit? What does this world have for me? What does God have for me? Where do family, friends, and dating fit? How important is it for me to connect to the local church?

Go back and review the topics addressed in each chapter under these themes. Think about what you can do to develop positive habits in each of these areas. Here are some steps to help you in the process:

Decide exactly what you want to do. In what area do you need to develop a new habit or change an old one? Maybe you want to nail down your identity and form holy habits, like Scripture study. You might decide to read a Psalm, a section from Proverbs, or a chapter from the gospel of Mark each day for the next several weeks. Maybe you need to prioritize your relationships or improve your study habits. Decide what habits you can develop to help you grow in the areas where you need to focus. Then write down those ideas and post them where you'll see them every day, like on your bathroom mirror, in your book bag, in your car, or in the shower. (If you choose the shower, don't forget to put them inside a Ziploc bag first!) Be as specific as possible; specific actions lead to specific habits.

Make time for what you want to do. Again, it takes around twenty-two days to form a habit, so schedule at least twenty-two days on your calendar and don't let anything get in the way. Schedule time with God. Schedule time for relationships. Schedule opportunities to have fun. Schedule, schedule, schedule. As you head into the real world, your time management will be completely dependent upon your keeping a good schedule. If you miss one of your scheduled days, don't stress out. Give yourself grace, but do your best to be consistent and dedicated to what you've decided to do so it can become a positive, God-honoring habit.

Encourage yourself. As you notice the action becoming a habit, congratulate yourself. But don't stop there. Keep going with the habit, but add another action for the next twenty-two days, then another, and so on, until you're doing those things you want to do as part of your daily routine without even thinking about them ... like brushing your teeth, riding a bike, sleeping (okay, maybe some of you need to develop this habit).

Finally, remember the goal: following Jesus. That's the point of these habits and the point of this book. My heart's desire has been to help you grow into mature Jesus-followers for the whole of your life. If you apply the principles of this book, you'll be well on your way.

Traps to Avoid

Take a deep breath—we're almost done. But before you close this book, I want to give you my list of the most common mistakes made by those who are leaving high school and entering the real world. These top-ten traps are in no particular order, but they all represent very real temptations for you to avoid as you head into this next chapter of your life. Stay alert and keep clear of these traps. Drumroll, please:

1. Listen more than you talk. Many leaving the high school world think they have it all figured out. I hope you've realized you don't have all the answers. Be careful to express your opinions and "expert advice" at the right times and in the right places. If you don't, you could find yourself in trouble with friends, coworkers, professors, church leaders, and others around you. Remember to listen more than you talk; this is proven to produce wisdom.

2. Exercise. It's vital for both your physical and your mental health. Some of you might have been active in high school, but many of you weren't all-star athletes. Start a habit of exercising immediately.

3. Draw healthy boundaries. Upon leaving high school, an overwhelming number of young people drop their moral boundaries and become sexually active. Don't put yourself in this position (literally)! Live for love, not lust. Set your boundaries now so you don't find yourself naked in the bed of someone you barely know. The consequences could send your life on a major detour for the worse. You don't want to go there.

4. Have fun. Seriously! College is about getting an education, preparing to join the workforce, and bringing home some cash; but these years are also about growing into a mature Jesus-follower for the rest of your life. This is a fun time, and God invented fun. So make sure you laugh and enjoy the abundant life he created for you to have in college and beyond.

5. Stay away from drugs. You'd think that being a follower of Jesus would dissuade one from using drugs. But like sex, the temptation to "experiment" will come at you in the real world like a pack of wild wolves pursuing a deer. Be on guard! Don't go down this path—you may think you can play around with this stuff safely, but you can easily become addicted and lose your relationships, job, and health. Drugs will destroy your life.

6. Eat healthy. Many leaving high school eat everything within arm's reach. Finally faced with the opportunity to make all of their own choices about food, they think they've died and gone to heaven. All-you-can-eat everything ... at ... every meal! It's great—until the second semester ends and they realize the reality of the "freshman fifteen." On the flipside, some students don't eat enough (or at all) and endanger their own health. Be wise in your eating habits: Your identity in Jesus is positively or negatively affected by them.

7. Don't abuse your freedom. Many who've recently been released from parental boundaries decide to party it up. They drink too much, do things they don't remember the next morning, and start down the path of destruction. Decide now that you won't put yourself in situations that can negatively affect your studies, class attendance, church participation, friendships, and overall health. You don't want this kind of reputation, especially as a Jesus-follower.

8. Avoid procrastination. Many wait till the last minute to get things done and fall behind. Maybe you got away with that kind of approach in high school, but it's time to wake up. In college and in the workforce, waiting till the last minute will get you failed or fired. Walking out of high school into the real world can be like stepping on a treadmill that's already moving 100 miles per hour. Be careful—you could get hurt. Once you're in the groove of college or the workforce, stay on pace so you don't get behind.

9. Stay involved. Many college-aged individuals sit in their dorm room or apartment when they're not in class or at work. It's hard to imagine, but some choose not to get involved in extracurricular activities. In college, there are plenty of things to do. There are many campus ministries and local churches to plug in to. The options are endless, so take advantage of your interests and stay active ... but balance them with studying and other activities.

10. Take Jesus with you. This one is the key. Many forget to take Jesus along when they leave high school. By this point in the book, I hope you understand the importance of making a relationship with the real Jesus a central part of your life. He loves you passionately and only wants the best for you. Follow him and let him guide your identity, choices, and belonging.

Finally ...

Not long ago, I was sitting at an airport gate in Chicago waiting for my next flight. I was just minding my own business when I clearly heard someone sing out, "Blessed be the Name of the Lord! Blessed be his Naaaammmmeee!" I looked up and saw a young guy bobbing his head to the music on his iPod, completely clueless of the volume level. The thirtysomething guy next to him turned and looked at the kid with an angry scowl on his face. But I noticed another guy standing between the rocking teenager and me. He had white hair and looked to be at least sixty years old. Our eyes met. He knew I'd heard the music and was smiling at me, shaking his head in approval as if to say, "That's a great tune! Blessed be his name!"

So here's my invitation to you as you begin this new season of life: As you leave high school, take that tune with you. Take Jesus with you for the long haul. God really is good. Think about the blessings he's given you: You can read, think, breathe, and eat. *You're alive.* God loves you regardless of what you've done and what challenges you face. Blessed be his name. As you grow older, don't become like that grumpy thirtysomething in the airport. Instead, take the music with you and crank it up. Keep bobbing your head to that beat till you're old and gray.

Well, this is the end of the book but the beginning of the rest of your life. May God unleash you into this world as an unstoppable force. May you bring his kingdom to earth as you move from surviving to thriving in your faith in Jesus.

Talk It Up!

Want free books?
First looks at the best new fiction?
Awesome exclusive merchandise?

We want to hear from you!

Give us your opinions on titles, covers, and stories.
Join the Z Street Team.

Visit zstreetteam.zondervan.com/joinnow
to sign up today!

Also—Friend us on Facebook!

www.facebook.com/goodteenreads

- Video Trailers
- Connect with your favorite authors
- Sneak peeks at new releases
- Giveaways
- Fun discussions
- And much more!

CPSIA information can be obtained
at www.ICGtesting.com
Printed in the USA
LVOW07s2247230617
539205LV00014B/349/P